Martin Chatterton and present

THE ULTIMATE
A-Z of FOOTY!

PUFFIN BOOKS

PUFFIN BOOKS

Penguin Books Ltd, 27 Wrights Lane, London W8 5TZ, England
Penguin Putnam Inc., 375 Hudson Street, New York, New York 10014, USA
Penguin Books Australia Ltd, Ringwood, Victoria, Australia
Penguin Books Canada Ltd, 10 Alcorn Avenue, Toronto, Ontario, Canada M4V 3B2
Penguin Books India (P) Ltd, 11 Community Centre, Panchsheel Park, New Delhi – 110 017, India
Penguin Books (NZ) Ltd, Cnr Rosedale and Airborne Roads, Albany, Auckland,
New Zealand
Penguin Books (South Africa) (Pty) Ltd, 5 Watkins Street, Denver Ext 4,
Johannesburg 2094, South Africa

On the World Wide Web at: www.penguin.com

Penguin Books Ltd, Registered Offices: Harmondsworth, Middlesex, England

First published 2001

1

Text and illustrations copyright © Martin Chatterton, 2001
Made and printed in England by Clays Ltd, St Ives plc
British Library Cataloguing in Publication Data
A CIP catalogue record for this book is available from the British Library

ISBN 0–141–31322–6

Featuring a star-studded cast of top footy types, including . . .

David Beckham!

Sir Alex Ferguson!

Peter Reid!

Alan Hansen!

Michael Owen!

Fabien Barthez!

David Seaman!

Abel Xavier!

Gary Lineker!

Frank Leboeuf!

Roy Keane!

and many, many, many more . . .

But first, a bit about your host for this evening . . .

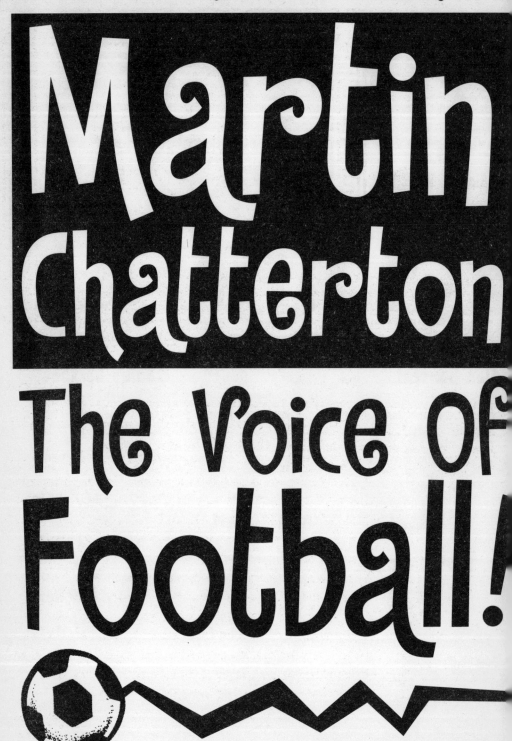

Martin Chatterton

The Voice of Football!

Born in humble surroundings, this son of concert violinists who had fallen on hard times, soon showed signs of the football talent which would take him almost as far as getting a trial for Everton FC. Only the petty jealousy of other players and a niggling Big Head problem prevented the young Chatterton from fulfilling his destiny as European football's premier marksman.

Instead, fuelled with desire for all things footy, and armed with his trusty pen and Macintosh G3 computer, Chatterton became the most famous and most respected authority on the beautiful game (that's football, for all you Aston Villa supporters).

Now in his prime at the age of about 30-ish, Chatterton is proud to wear the title of 'The Voice of Football' with, er, pride. The dashing good looks and astonishing football skills are still clear to see as Chatterton completes ten years at the top. He is married to a devoted wife, Ann, who thinks he's chuffin' brill, and has two wonderful children, Sophie and Danny, who hang on his every word. When not writing and illustrating he is to be found patrolling his beloved 10,000-acre coastal estate at Chatterton Towers in Little-Southport-by-the-Sea.

OK. That's all the guff. Let's get on with the book . . .

It's a funny old game, isn't it? Croquet, that is. And lacrosse, there's another funny old game. As are golf, curling, pelota, cricket, rugby and bowls.

Football, on the other hand, is deadly serious and this is *the* book you'll need if you are going to get up to speed with everything that's worth knowing in the wonderful world of footy.

We've got lots of laughs (in fact we gorra lorra lorra laffs), lots of facts, quizzy questions and groovy pics. Perfect for filling in the time between Saturday afternoon and, er, Sunday afternoon.

A stupid person reading this book, your dad or younger sister, for example, might be confused about which stories are true and which stories aren't. Mainly cos we've mixed the lot up, and it's in a right old state, let me tell you.

So, we've come up with a cunning plan.

When you see this symbol you'll know that this bit is solid gold and *true*.

When you see this symbol you'll know that this is just some tosh we made up for a laff and is, in fact, total *pants*.

One word of warning before you get reading: I have a tragic confession to make. I am an Everton supporter. There, I've said it. I don't feel I've got anything to be ashamed of, I just thought it might explain the odd outburst of ToffeeMania sprinkled throughout this magnificent book.

A is for...

Ability

Here's a strange thing: there are only about 2,000 professional footy players in the UK, right? However, if you ask any bloke about your dad's age they'll all say the same thing. 'Oh, yeah. I had trials for Man United/Arsenal/Inter Milan/Brazil but I couldn't be bothered with all that so I gave up and became Assistant Deputy Trolley Controller for Tesco in Swindon. I had the *ability*, of course, but no luck.'

ABANDONED!

It's quite rare nowadays for matches to be abandoned, but it does still happen every so often. A game at West Ham was abandoned in 1999 after somebody tinkered with the floodlights and plunged the game into darkness.

These days, the match is replayed in full, but in them olden days, when your dad was in black and white and everything cost nothing, teams were only allowed to play the time remaining when the match was abandoned! This was stopped after a number of replayed matches lasted only five minutes.

Spare a thought for how the players of Birmingham City felt when their game against Darlaston was abandoned with less than 30 minutes left. The score: Birmingham 16, Darlaston 0 ...

ALIENS!

For some time now the FA Deep Space Probe has been gathering information from, erm, deep space, and relaying it back to the top-secret footy radar listening posts situated on some boggy bit of windswept moorland somewhere in the north of England. Trained footy scientists have picked up high-pitched, coded-frequency messages, which have revealed a number of our footballers are, in fact, slimy alien creatures from outer space (and France).

The FA Deep Space Probe passing the second Moon of Nebula 6

Think about it; Michael Owen's unnatural calm in front of goal, his robotic stare, his 'niceness' show all the signs of him being . . . an android! *An android programmed to become so popular it would take over the world given half a chance!*

Owen . . . or *Android?*

A rare sighting of the Beckham maintenance hatch

David Beckham, or ZX-564744432, as he is known on the Planet Tharg, is another example. Hardly ever gets interviewed, probably because his human voice decoder is faulty. Covers himself in tattoos to hide the maintenance-hatch covers on his skin. Married Posh (the female android who infiltrated the Spice Girls) to complete Phase One of the Emperor of Tharg's plan to swamp the planet with stories about the Beckhams, driving us all into a coma.

His Mightiness, the Emperor Tharg

And Frank LeBoeuf, is, we can exclusively reveal, none other than His Mightiness himself, Lord of All the Outer Galaxies and Protector of the Ninth Quadrant, the Emperor Tharg! Despite the chance that he might be spotted as an alien, the Emperor is too vain to use a wig to cover up his shining head, which is a sign of importance back home on Planet Tharg.

ANGRY!

There are many, many candidates for the angriest player ever. Patrick 'It Weren't Me, Guv, Honest' Viera of Arsenal and France; Roy 'Prawn Sandwich' Keane, the shaven-headed Man U captain; Billy Bremner, the ex-Leeds, ginger-top mid-fielder; Alan Smith, the babyface Leeds striker Norman 'Bites Yer Legs' Hunter, also of Leeds. And how about every-one's fave bad boy, David 'Gets Sent off in a Very Important World Cup Match for Being a Bit Tetchy and Kicking Someone' Beckham?

We liked Jack Charlton, ex of Leeds (lot of Leeds players in this; funny that, isn't it?), England and ex-Ireland manager, talking about his lack of calm when it came to footy: 'I'm very placid most of the time, but I blow up very quickly, I shout and wave my arms around and my lip twitches.'

Big Jack, who used to be a fearsome centre half in a wild-tackling Leeds side also had this to say about his opponents: 'I've got a little black book in which I keep the names of all the players I've got to get before I pack up playing. If I get half a chance they will finish up over the touchline.'

Anthems (National)

This is normally the bit in a big match when you pop out to the loo, or, if you are watching at home, get up to fetch some more Pringles. But you are missing out on some top fun. Watching the teams attempt to sing the national anthem can be one of the most rewarding sights in modern football if you are really sad and have no life whatsoever. Just take a look at the way that all the players look like they are appearing in a badly dubbed movie. Their lips are moving but not in time with the music. And they haven't got a clue about the words.

Astroturf

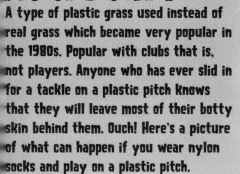

A type of plastic grass used instead of real grass which became very popular in the 1980s. Popular with clubs that is, not players. Anyone who has ever slid in for a tackle on a plastic pitch knows that they will leave most of their botty skin behind them. Ouch! Here's a picture of what can happen if you wear nylon socks and play on a plastic pitch.

Away Games

It's obviously a disadvantage to have to play at an opponent's ground. All those nasty fans shouting rude things at you, cold dressing rooms and a long journey before the game. Sometimes it's all too much: on one match day in 1937, all thirty-five League and Cup matches ended without an away win. In 1990/91, Hibernian lost EVERY away game they played.

And all that travelling can make a difference. Carlisle, stuck oop north, have to travel more than most. A trip to Exeter or any other southerly side can mean a nine- or ten-hour drive. Of course, teams higher up the league can afford to fly. Unless players are scared of flying, like Dennis Bergkamp, who drives for *two whole days* to get to away games.

Beckham 'The Brain'

It's a little known fact, what we made up, that the squeaky-voiced, fashion victim that most people think of as David Beckham is also one of the leading scientists in the very brainy subject of Hard Sums and Intergalactic Molecular Genetic Fusion Studies! Yes! Becks secretly studied all this gubbins in the afternoons after training, and on those long flights to European away

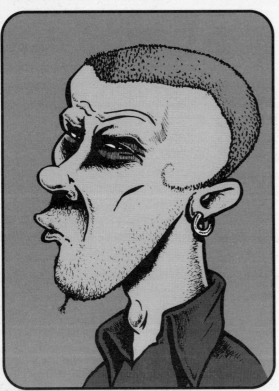

games. All the brainy book-reading increased his intelligence so much that he had to shave off his floppy fringe to let his mighty brain cool down!

Now Becks can hardly find the time to slot bendy free kicks into the top left-hand corner, what with leading university blokes and scientists queueing outside the dressing room to ask his advice . . .

BEEF

Beef plays a surprisingly large part in the unheard story of footy. Well, actually it plays hardly any part at all but I thought I'd give it a bit of a build-up.

Amazing Beef Fact 1.

Coventry City's Moroccan maestro Moustapha Hadji liked beef so much that he strapped a bit of it to his foot and played for two months during the 1999/2000 season. It wasn't that he was injured, he just liked really tender beef. Like, *really* tender.

Amazing Beef Fact 2.

Chubby cricket commentator Ian 'Beefy' Botham played cricket for Somerset and England at the same time as he was turning out for the mighty Scunthorpe.

Amazing Beef Fact 3.

Er, there is no Amazing Beef Fact 3. Oh, hold on, Ron Radford scored a famous goal for Hereford United to knock Newcastle out of the cup and Hereford is a breed of cow, isn't it?

Amazing Beef Fact 4.

Ion Radu of Romanian bottom feeders Jiul Petrosani was sold to Vicea for 1,200 pounds of beef in 1998.

Boots

Back in them olden days, before the dawn of Sky TV, the Premiership and David Beckham, boots were sturdy, black objects, caked in mud and weighing about 450 kilos each. It took three years to soften the rock-hard leather and during this 'running-in' period it was like playing with ski boots on.

In the 1970s there were oddball experiments with swivel plates in the soles, white boots, side-lacing boots, all a load of old malarkey if you ask us.

1. White boots proved useless in snowy conditions.

2. Swivel boots caused medical problems.

3. Side-lacing boots were fine but just looked a bit girly really.

Now, in today's modern cut-and-thrust game, boots are changing beyond all recognition. Blades instead of studs, rippled leather insteps, lightweight polymer soles, silicon-heel buffers . . . the list goes on. All well and good.

However, what we at *The Ultimate A-Z of Footy* want is an immediate ban on silver and gold boots. Red, green, blue and yellow are all bad enuff. But when we see our fave players flouncing on to the pitch looking like they are wearing a pair of shiny ballet slippers it's time for us to shout:

Oi! YOU LOT! STOP!

Brazilian Ball Skills

One of the greatest players in the world, gap-toothed Brazilian Ronaldo, is well known for his amazing ball control. But in 1999 he met someone who could match him: his girlfriend Milene Domingues, who held the world record for 'keepy-up'. In 1995 she had kicked the ball 55,187 times without it touching the floor. It took her an unbelievable nine hrs six minutes . . .

With so much money to be won betting on football games, it's not surprising that some people will stop at nothing to 'fix' the result by paying players to play badly, or to 'throw' a game as it is better known.

Football has had its fair share of dodgy money changing hands. As far back as 1913, one stingy player offered a fiver to each player in high-flying West Bromwich Albion (shows you how long ago it was) to 'throw' their upcoming game.

Fortunately the Baggies captain, Jessie (stop sniggering at the back, Perkins!) Pennington, foiled the dastardly plot and turned the crook over to the cops. Hurrah!

Two years later even the mighty Man Utd and Liverpool were under suspicion when nine players were suspended after 'fixing' matches so that they could win heavily by betting on the results.

Based in the whiffy east coast fishing port, Grimsby Town (nicknamed, strangely enough, 'The Codheads') used to give gifts of boxes of fish to opponents. But the League stopped them in 1945 on the grounds that it was . . . well, a bit fishy.

C is for...

Cricket

Ancient, stunningly, blindingly, ridiculously BORING 'game'. There's no actual story here, I just thought I'd put it in because that's the kind of guy I am. As for golf, well, don't start me on that . . .

Champions of the World!

Strangely enough, the first Champions of the World weren't Uruguay, who won the first ever World Cup. No, the very first title of 'Champions of the World' went to mighty Renton FC of the Scottish League in 1888, after they had beaten the English FA Cup winners, West Brom. They were given the title by the promoters of the match, who figured that, as British teams were obviously the best, it stood to reason that the winners of this game would be the best in the world . . . In 1954, even more strangely, Stan Cullis, the manager of Wolverhampton Wanderers, made the claim that, in fact, Wolves were 'The Champions of the World', after they had beaten Honved and Moscow Spartak! To be fair, Moscow and Honved *were* two of the teams most feared in world football at the time, but still . . .

Corner Flags

Bits of wood with dinky little flags attached placed in each corner of footy pitches. Why? Because referees can't tell where the pitch stops and the stadium begins. Knowing the average referee's eyesight as we do, we'd like to suggest another design for corner flags (see fig. 1).

fig. 1

Comics!

We all have our fave footy comic characters, Roy of The Rovers being the most famous. My personal choice would be Gorgeous George, a goalkeeper, fabulously rich, who turned up for games in a Rolls-Royce, chauffeur-driven on to the pitch. George was incredibly brainy and could spot exactly where a ball was going *before* a forward hit it. On a free kick, for example, he might position himself right away from the goal, leaving it open, because George knew that when the player hit the ball, it would rebound to him and he could throw it straight to his forwards to score. He would also leave games early because he'd judge that the opposition would never score in the time available. What a star.

Note: for copyright reasons mainly but also coz we can't be bothered, we are unable to show the picture of Gorgeous George. Pity, because it was really fab . . .

COWPATS

Not normally associated with the modern game, you could be fooled into thinking that cowpats are a thing of the past. Not so! Just last Saturday I came a right cropper when slipping on one just as I was shaping for a nice half-volley. Of course, give me cowpats over doggy doo any day . . .

13

The Champions League

Roy Keane holds the controversial new Champions League Trophy.

My dictionary says that a champion is 'someone who has beaten all others in a competition'. So what's going on in that Champions League, eh? Not only do we get the actual champions of every country, we get teams who finished second, third and even fourth! So the real name should be The Champions, Runners-up, Third-placed and More Or Less Any Old Tat Who Managed to Scrape a Few Points Together League. Thank you.

Carrot

Mad-as-a-brush Brazilian striker Edmilson scored for his side Atletico Mineiro against local rivals 'America'. Yes, 'America'.

To celebrate his strike, Edmilson did what any self-respecting goalscorer would do. That's right, he whipped a carrot from his shorts and started to eat it in front of the opposing supporters. Well, you would, wouldn't you?

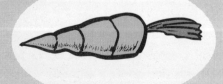

Coracle

A small, roundish boat made of waterproofed hides, which dates back to them olden days, does not seem to have any connection with footy. But if you thought that you'd be wrong.

Fred Davies sat in a coracle on the River Severn every Saturday afternoon for forty-five years, fishing out footballs kicked out of Shrewsbury Town's ground, which is next to the river. He was paid about thirty pence a ball and rescued thousands of them over the years before retiring in 1986 at the age of seventy-five.

CHIMP

1. Chimpanzee

This is a picture of a chimpanzee.

2. Peter Reid

This is a picture of Peter Reid, ex-Everton and England player and Sunderland boss.

There's no particular reason why we put these pictures next to each other. That's our story and we're sticking to it. Cheer up, Peter Reid!

D is for...

DINOSAURS!

It's common knowledge that dinosaurs have been extinct for more than 65 million years. But startling new pictures show that a few of these magnificent creatures managed to survive and find a home in today's world of foot

Here's the Big Daddy of 'em all, **Tyrannosaurus Ref.** A large, aggressive meat eater, Tyrannosaurus Ref hunts alone. He thinks nothing of red carding at will, gobbling up as many as four or five players in one game. If cornered by a T. Ref, stand perfectly still they have terrible eyesight, responding only to movement or Manchester United manage

This is the **Volleyciraptor**, a quick, agile dinosaur who usually plays up front, or just behind the strikers as an attacking midfielder. Has good ball skills, excellent vision and, as the name suggests, loves cracking 'em in from just outside the box before the ball touches the ground.

Threetimesayearotops is a short-lived, multi-coloured creature, much loved by young collectors who just must have each type of Threetimesayearotops, no matter what the cost. Some say that it's the big clubs who breed these desirable creatures simply to make loads of cash.

The Dippydocus (Paulusgascoigneus) is a huge, slow-moving, near-extinct, midfield creature with distinctive, highly coloured markings. Can be recognized by its loud, honki noise. The Dippydocus has a brain the size of a walnut and injury-prone legs. Its surviva thought to be because of its amazingly agile feet which help get it out of trouble. Not related to the equally dim, but talented, Verydippydocus (Nikolanelkaus).

The easily angered **Dicaniosaurus** can be spotted by its typical white feet, astonishing speed and readiness to take on Tyrannosaurus Ref in one-to-one combat.

Diet

Today's fresh, clean, modern celebrity footy player eats lots and lots of healthy green stuff, nuts and pasta and only drinks pure mountain-spring water. But it wasn't always like this. In the dim and distant past, proper footballers ate proper food, like fried eggs, chips, beans, pies, black pudding, tripe, cake, fried bread, sausages, more pies and washed it all down with a bucket of stewed tea sweetened with forty-three sugars. And that was just breakfast.

The league-championship-winning Old Bootonians of 1884 ate nothing but fried sheep's stomach linings and trifle for an entire season. The manager swore blind by the diet but Old Bootonians never won another championship. All but two of the squad, faced with the prospect of another season of fried belly, cream and fruit, legged it down the road to sign for Arsenal. Arsenal followed a proper pre-match diet of a four-course roast dinner, with all the trimmings, and attracted more players because of it

A typical pre-match meal for Arsenal 1899

Dodgy Debuts

Imagine the pride a player feels when he trots on to the pitch to make his very, very first appearance for a professional club. He will dream of scoring three in thirteen minutes, like Fred Howard who went on to notch four in his first game for Man City against Liverpool. Or like Tony Coton, the keeper who saved a penalty with his very first touch in league football, playing for Birmingham City.

Imagine how that player must feel though, if his debut is as dodgy as some of these . . .

Les Surnam, making a 1965 start for Charlton Athletic in goal, let three goals in and NEVER played for them again. Dennis Murray, also a keeper, let NINE in for Crewe Alexandra in his first game. But all this pales into nothing compared with the debut of Steve Milton. Playing in goal for Halifax Town in 1934, Milton had THIRTEEN walloped past him. Oh dear.

In the 2000/20001 season, Mark Viduka of Leeds scored one of the quickest ever Premiership goals, in just eleven seconds . . .

Diving

The art of pretending to be fouled so that you'll fool the referee into giving a penalty. British commentators seem to think that it's only foreign players who do this, but we have this amazing picture of Munchester United's Frimley Scrimshaw taking a dive during the 1998 Cup Final.

E is for...

EXPLODING MANAGERS!

'Great bunch of lads', 'The lads are gutted', 'The lads are over the moon'. All common phrases used by our beloved manager types. But did you know that overuse of the word 'lads' can cause widespread injury and even death?! Read on . . .

Ex-England boss and full-time Toon Army manager Sir Bobby of Robson was once clocked at an amazing 146 lpi (saying 'lads' 146 times per interview) shortly after a victory over Man Utd. During the interview after a hot August Charity Shield game, Sir Bobson went haywire. Only on-the-spot emergency surgery to remove the portion of his brain that dealt with saying 'lads', saved him from exploding all over Wembley. Sir Bobs kindly donated his brain to the Scientific Footy Research Institute where it has been studied by top footy boffins (see fig. 3). Hopefully, with this kind of dedicated behind-the-scenes research, the risk of exploding managers will become a thing of the past.

Fig. 3: Top boffins study Sir Bobson's brain in an anti-gravity chamber.

Eggs

Grimsby goalie Aidan Davison has gone right off eggs after being knocked out cold by an egg thrown during a game at Fulham in 1998. Which reminds me . . .
Which team does Humpty Dumpty support?
Eggs-eter City . . . (Oh, stop, my aching sides . . .)

EVERTON! EVERTON! EVERTON!

Are, in fact, the greatest team the world has ever seen. Blue is the colour, football is the game, we're all together and winning is our aim. Come on, you blue boys! School of Scienc . . . ('OK Mr Chatterton, just slip your arms into the nice straitjacket and these nice men in nice white coats will take you somewhere nice and quiet . . .')

Eton

...ad posh school what claims it invented ...oty except they called it the Eton Wall ...me. So, if the toffs had had *their* way, the ...rious game of footy would, in fact, be the ...rious game of, erm ... Wally. Proof, if any ...re needed, that these chinless wonders ...ve no place in The People's Game.
...on, clear off, Tarquin Fotherington-Smythe!

Excuses

'Sorry I'm late, sir, my dad's car was attacked by a herd of wild buffalo while we were driving to school.'

You wouldn't expect your teech to swallow that load of old trip would you? Yet footballers and clubs think nothing of spouting loads of this stuff for their excuses.

Check these out . . .

The manager of Chelsea in 1999 was late for a meeting with the press. The excuse? 'Mr Vialli is shaving his head.'

Alex Ferguson's worst buy, Italian keeper Massimo 'Loose Gloves' Taibi, fluffed an easy shot through his legs in September 1999. His excuse? 'My studs were too long.'

'Springy balls' were the reason that Reading lost to Oxford in November 1999, according to boss Alan Pardew.

Another goalie, Argentinian Carlo Roa, decided in June 1999 that he would quit playing at the early age of twenty-nine. His excuse? T world was going to end in Januar 2000.

But perhaps the most famous footy excuse ever was that of Diego Maradona who, playing against England in the 1986 World Cup quarter final, and unseen by the referee, punched the ball into the net to knock England out. His excuse? It wasn't him punching the ball, it was 'The Hand of God'.

ELK

Driving home one evening, chubby Swedish former international Tomas Brolin, ex of Leeds and Parma, was involved in a collision with an elk. The massive hairy beast, weighing an estimated two tons, was travelling at around thirty miles per hour when he hit the poor elk.

Extra Time

It's up to the ref exactly how much time he or she adds on to make up for wasted time. Clive 'The Book' Thomas, the infamous Welsh referee, once added a mindboggling extra forty-five minutes to a match! In the days before penalty shoot-outs, matches sometimes had to go on being played until someone scored a goal. This meant that in 1946 Stockport and Doncaster Rovers played a cup match which lasted almost THREE AND A HALF HOURS! With the scores level at 4-4 the game dragged on, and on, and on. Large numbers of the crowd left to have their evening meal and then returned to find the match still being played! Eventually bad light stopped the game and a replay was ordered.

THE FERGUSON EFFECT

Everyone knows, even Liverpool and Man City supporters, that Manchester United have been the greatest team in Britain for a long, long time. Come on, admit it, they are, aren't they? The reason? Their manager, Alex Ferguson. How does he do it? Well, by a grasp of tactics second to none, training, man management, building up a pool of talent, investing wisely on the transfer market and ... *by being The Scariest Manager in Football!!!!!*

All managers need to have some steel in their gaze, something which chills the bones of any player who catches it. But Fergie is surely the greatest at this.

Last month after their first home defeat in
2,036,754 United home games, a hideous wreck
of a man was found wandering deep in the
bowels of the main stand.

White-haired and wild-eyed, he gibbered out
a story that made grown men scream like
Barbie-doll-playing nellies, and grown women
faint dead away. It is a tale of terror so pant-
wettingly scary that we have to ask children
under seven to leave the book now. Have they
gone?

Very well. You have been warned.

The man in our story was Phully Loaded, a
new pitch-side reporter for the BBC.

United were losing 1-0 and the
referee blew his whistle.

Instantly a chill settled across
the ground, the United players
sank to their knees, some wailing,
and yea others did rend their very
garments.

A few, a brave few, cast wary
glances towards the dugout, where
a tall figure stood, seemingly
calm, but a closer look revealed
him to be vibrating at high speed.

Lasers shot from his eyes, scorching the green turf and inflicting second-degree burns on players unfortunate enough to cross his path.

An eerie, alien sound came from the figure's mouth which had the crowd clamping hands over ears. The sound, like a chainsaw in a china shop, was the figure's teeth being ground. Fragments of enamel fell from his lips.

It was at this moment that Phully Loaded made his fatal mistake. Approaching the figure, he waved his microphone at The Gaffer (for it was He) and asked The Last Question He Would Ever Ask.

Ferg, looked like that was a well-deserved victory for Everton. Why do you think the ref played so much time added on?

The next thing the reporter remembered was waking up in a medieval dungeon, strapped to a torture rack and being jabbed with sharpened forks. He was only released after his brain had been rinsed clean of all anti-United thought and he had sworn a blood oath of allegiance to all things Red and White.

Now Phully can't get enough of the jolly little Red Devils. He's become a season ticket holder and never misses a United game, home or away. He can't remember much about what happened to him, but if you should ever come across a man in a Man Utd shirt with a silly grin on his mush . . . No, hold on, there's loads of them, aren't there? If you should ever come across a man with 'My Name is Phully Loaded and I Love Man U!' on his T-shirt, just get right up close and whisper one word to him: 'Ferguson' and watch as he leaps ten feet straight up in the air.

So, there it is. Traveller beware! When approaching a Fergie, make certain you have adequate protective clothing, a change of trousers and undercrackers and a taxi, revved-up and waiting. Otherwise, you too could end up like Phully Loaded in today's spine-tingling, scary story . . .

Of course, this is all just so much wibbly-wobbly nonsense. The real Manchester United and Alex Ferguson are nothing like this and would never have anything to do with anything nasty. In fact, here's a picture of Sir Alex cuddling his favourite teddy, Wilson.

Fans

We all want to see our fave team win and true fans try their best to attend most games. Some people, however, take things a little too far . . . Check out this lot:

In 1998/99 footy fan Ebby Kleinrensing spent over £15,000 travelling to watch all Nottingham Forest's home games . . . from her house in Düsseldorf, Germany!

Bob Steer, a Brighton fan, decided to watch Brighton make their 1977 First Division debut rather than go to . . . his son's wedding! And spare a thought for little Baby Waterfield, born in 1999. Her mum, Diane from Margate, knew exactly what to call her . . . Manchester!

Little Bearsdley Dixon playing happily.

Mind you, Manchester Waterfield probably got off lightly compared to Beardsley Dixon and Dalglish Dixon. Both girls were unlucky enough to have Newcastle United fans for parents. Never mind, they can always grow up and marry one of the three sons of Manchester United fan Jason Villette: Ince Villette, Cantona Villette or Beckham Villette.

Some Sheffield Wednesday supporters are rumoured not to eat bacon, because the red and white stripes remind them of the hated Sheffield United shirt . . .

Newcastle fan Dominic Hurd was so upset at a last-minute winner for Liverpool against his side that he kicked out at the nearest object: the pole for his budgie's cage. The bird died of shock, leaving Dom sick as a parrot . . .

Forfar

Scottish club who have never really done much in their long history. But we like them when they play East Fife, because there's always the chance of the scoreline reading:
'Forfar four, East Fife five.'

Flowers Of Scotland

In the 1900 Scotland win over England, Scotland played in the unlikely colours of primrose and pink.

FOG!

In the 1940s, goalie Sam Bartram, playing for Charlton during a game in thick fog, had to be told by a passing policeman that the game had been abandoned and all the other players were back in the dressing room.

31

G is for...

Goalkeepers!

Where *do* we start?

The undisputed kings of comedy, it's a scientific fact, proven by brainy boffins what know what they is talking about, that all goalies are one sandwich short of a picnic.

It's easy to figure out why. Goalies are often left alone on the pitch for long periods of time. Sometimes (if you play for Manchester United for example) it's possible to spend the entire season completely cut off from human contact.

It's a strong rumour, made up by me, that Peter Schmeichel didn't crack in being the Man U keeper to play for Lisbon. He was, in fact, rescued by a crack team of Goalkeeping Veterans and is currently undergoing treatment in the Swiss Goalkeeping Madness Treatment Centre before being slowly reintroduced into society.

His case came to their attention when he cracked during a Man U European tie against Rotor Volgograd, legged it up the field, screaming like a demented Dane, and scored with a header.

was obvious that something had to be done.

Since Schmeichel left, few have been able to stand the loneliness at Old Trafford: Raymond Van Der Gouw, Francesco Tabbia, Mark Bosnich and Fabian Barthez have all tried to live with life as a Red goalie.

Barthez copes by trying to take throw-ins, free kicks, even shooting at the opponent's goal. During games against lower-division sides he actually takes a laptop on to the field to carry on writing his novel, *The Loneliness of the Old Trafford Goalkeeper.*

There have been *so* many loopy goalkeeping stories that we have pick just a few to illustrate these pages.

How about Bert Trautmann, Manchester City's German goalie in the 1950s? He played almost all of the 1956 FA Cup Final after *breaking his neck* during the game.

It's OK, boss, it's just a flesh wound . . .

r what about Brucie Grobelaar,
e ex-commando who played for
iverpool until the mid-1990s? He
nce faced up to the final penalty
n a European Cup Final pretending
o have wobbly legs; or how about
ne time he opened an umbrella to
nelter from the rain during a
ame at Anfield? Or even his habit
° taking to the pitch walking on
is hands?

Bruce prepares to face the deciding
penalty against Roma.

Or John Beresford, the ex-Coventry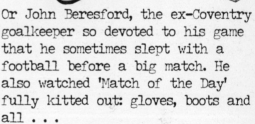
goalkeeper so devoted to his game
that he sometimes slept with a
football before a big match. He
also watched 'Match of the Day'
fully kitted out: gloves, boots and
all . . .

 Roberto Rojas, the cheating
ilean keeper, who famously cut
mself with a hidden scalpel and
etended that he'd been hit by a
ssile from the crowd so that
ile would get the points in their
rld Cup game against Brazil?

Gentlemen

In the early days of footy, when players had big whiskery whiskers and played in top hats and frock coats, the game was divided into 'gentlemen', who were amateurs (that means they weren't paid to play) and 'players' (who were paid). The 'gentlemen' were usually snooty, stiff-upper-lippers, strolling onto the field, hands behind back. 'Players', on the

Lord Ffilllip Arthur Bumcheek of Rutland, centre forward for Aston Villonia, 1879

other hand, were honest-to-goodness working blokes, who were looked down upon by the snooty 'gentlemen'.

Alf Pipe, fullback for Coalpit Wanderers, 1884

Things have changed a lot since then, but you can still get booked for 'ungentlemanly conduct' today.

One of the best-known 'gentlemen' teams were Corinthians, who formed in 1882. They were a bunch of toffee-nosed snobs, but you do have to admire their style. If a Corinthian player gave away a penalty, the Corinthian goalie would stand next to a goalpost, allowing the penalty to roll into an empty net. This was because as 'gentlemen' they couldn't stand the idea of saving the penalty – as it would mean they had 'got away' with cheating! On the other hand, if a Corinthian player got a penalty, he would deliberately miss, because he refused to believe a 'gentleman' would deliberately trip an opponent up!

GOAL!

Everyone loves a game with lots of goals. Th record for a game in England is 26-0 for Preston against Hyde in 1887. In Scotland it' the 36-0 demolition of Bon Accord by the mighty Arbroath in 1885. A more recent gam in Argentina ended 71-0 after one of the sid went on a sit-down strike on the pitch.

But would you really like to have seen the game played by the Indian Boys Athletic Association of Calcutta in 1983 where the final score was 114-0! To make matters worse the game only lasted seventy minutes. That's a goal every thirty-seven seconds . . .

The match that tops all others is the 1979 Yugoslavian title decider which finished 134-1. It was later found out that one of the teams had been paid to 'influence' the resu

George Simpkins ...
The Guffer

No. 1 in a series of Unsung Footy Greats

The Great George 'Guffer' Simpkins, rumoured to be the smelliest player ever to take to a football pitch. Guffer, although totally untalented as a player, nevertheless played at centre half for Leyton Orient shortly after the Second World War (big war about fifty years ago, look it up, dim-wit). In eighty-seven games he never had a goal scored by any player he was marking. This was mainly because they passed into a three-week coma shortly after getting a whiff of the Guffer's body aroma.

His technique was to do close, man-to-man marking, making skilful use of his pongy bod, which had been described as 'like a rancid old skunk's mattress left out in the rain'. His run of form with Orient would have continued if it hadn't been for the petition his own teammates collected asking the club to get rid of him. 'The fumes I breathed in when playing behind Simpkins for almost two seasons, have left me with serious health problems in later life,' said wheezing ex-Orient keeper, Scuffly Clearance.

H is for...

Hacking

When football was beginning to become an organized game, players were allowed to kick an opponent in the legs! Broken bones were frequent and the FA eventually banned 'hacking' as it was known.

Hair

Cor blimey! There have been so many footballing hair horrors down the years (the 'Bobby Charlton' comb-over, the 'Kev Keegan' bubble perm, the 'Beckham' flop), that it's silly to dredge them all up again. Instead we salute the entire Romanian team who dyed their hair bright yellow before their vital 1998 World Cup quarter final.

Heading

The skill of using your noggin to move the ball. There have been some great headers of the ball down the years, usually goalscorers. In 1952 Peter Aldis scored for Aston Villa against Sunderland with a header from a distance of thirty-two metres!

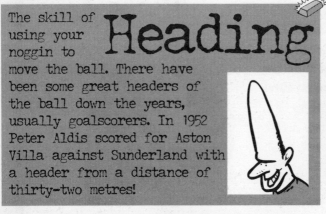

Half Time

'It's a game of two 'alves, innit?' says Ron Manager time and time again. But what about the bit in the middle, the half-time interval? Have you ever wondered just what goes on in the dressing room at half-time? We've gone behind the scenes at two locations: compare a Premiership club and a Division 2 (West) Preston & District game.

Hoofing It

The ancient and dying art of wellying the ball high into Row Z. We all expect our defenders to combine the ball skills of Luis Figo with the football brain of, er, Luis Figo, and stroke the ball about the pitch. I must admit I've got a soft spot for those central defenders whose motto is 'When in doubt, smack it out'. You do see it more often in the amateur game, but I still like it when our top players give it some welly and the crowd make donkey noises.

Some less-skilled players than myself sometimes fluff easy chances instead of coolly drilling them into the top left-hand corner of the net, 1-0! Chatterton has scored and the crowd go wild!!! FRRRRRRRWWWWWAAAAAAHHHH!

Sorry, where was I? Oh, howlers. The most famous fluff ever was the one by Gordon Smith in the dying seconds of the 1983 FA Cup Final when playing for Brighton against Manchester United. Clean through on goal with the score at 1-1, the commentator yelled out 'And Smith must score!' He didn't.

HYPNOTISM

From time to time, footy managers have taken the desperate step of sending for a hypnotist to help their team win.

I played for a team that was hypnotized once. We had lost forty-three games in a row, conceding 238 goals and scoring just four. The manager brought in El Mysterioso, a top hypnotist from just down the road and set him to work. He took us all into a dark room, looked deep into our eyes and chanted 'You will win, you will win', over and over again.

We were playing the team at the top of the league that afternoon and we took to the pitch full of steely confidence. And do you know what happened? We got hammered 9-0. But I did do a cracking impersonation of a dog, and Phil, the left back, pretended he was playing the violin.

I is for...

The Imp in the Penalty Box

A relative of the jolly little fairy folk who live at the bottom of my garden, the Irish Leprechaun and the Scandinavian Troll, the Penalty Box Imp lives behind the goalposts and is invisible to most people.

The Imp likes nothing better than to wait until a talented, dashing, striker (me, for example) appears in the penalty box. The Imp will wait until I've gone round the centre half, skipped past the keeper and have only to side-foot a dead easy shot to score the winner, before nipping out from his hidey-hole, tying me bootlaces together and laughing hysterically as I fluff it wide of the right-hand post. It wasn't me, it was The Imp. That's my story and I'm sticking to it. (See page 22 'Excuses'.)

Of course, all top-flight goalscorers are blessed with full ImpVision and can see the little blighters before they can do their evil.

40

Intelligence and Football

Top footy boffins have been examining the effect of footy on the intelligence of humans and have come up with a pile of completely startling, and yet totally untrue, tosh on the subject.

Here is a picture of a normal brain.

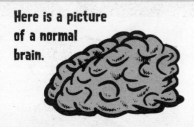

Here is a picture of the brain of someone who watches a lot of football.

You can clearly see that watching footy makes your brain smaller. Or so it seems. My brain, in fact, is twice as large as any Liverpool FC supporter. Clear evidence that Everton are better than Liverpool and all other teams, I think you'll agree.

Paul Diffling

The boffins also checked out the head of Paul Diffling, Scunthorpe's only fan, and made an amazing discovery: absolutely no brain at all! On second thoughts, perhaps that's not so difficult to believe.

It was when the research team began to look at players and managers that some of the most interesting brain facts came out.

Here's a top-secret scan of the inside of Sven Goran Ericksonn's head. As you can see, the crafty Swede is, in fact, controlled by little people who live inside his head and operate a high-powered super Swedish computer!

And this is what happened when our scientists opened up a hatch on the side of the great Sir Alex Ferguson's head while he was sleeping. You can see that he generates enough energy to power a small nuclear submarine.

Ing-er-land

Strange football-mad country supported by odd-looking, shaven-headed, Teletubby blokes in white shirts, usually found to be chanting the name of their side over and over again: 'Inge-er-land! Ing-e-rland! Ing-er-land!'

Strangely, Ingerland never seem to win anything, but the Ing-er-land supporters think that they are great!

Ipswich Town Football Club

Come on then, where *is* Ipswich?

Based in one of the most mysterious and least explored places on earth, this footy club has produced two managers who went on to lead England (Sir Alf Ramsey and Sir Bobby of Robson: see page 22 'Exploding Managers') and has also won the League, the FA Cup and the UEFA Cup. However, our top experts have discovered that Ipswich does not, in fact, exist! We can find no one who has ever been there, no one is sure of exactly where it is (it appears in different places on different maps) and, er, that's it.

Of course, I'm sure we'll get the odd crank letter from people claiming they actually *live* in Ipswich, or went there once to play 'em in a second-round, second-leg AutoWindshield Trophy away game in 1982, but we'll be handing these over to the FBI for examination. (STOP PRESS!!! IPSWICH ARE ACTUALLY PRETTY GOOD. SHOCK! AUTHOR APOLOGIZES!)

Italy

ickeningly good at winning
ooty matches, the Italian team are
ne of the very best international
eams there has ever been. However,
e have developed a plan for upset-
ing these mobile fashion victims
he next time your team plays them.

Tip 1: Persuade your players to ruffle the Italian players' hair. This will cause them to scream hysterically and rush from the field to find a mirror and comb.

ip 2: Sneak into the group of
hotographers wearing an orange
uorescent jacket with the name of
top fashion mag, like *Vogue*
rinted on it. Then stand slightly
vay from the goal. All the
alian players will slow down
nen they see you so you can
hotograph their best side,
abling your defenders to tackle 'em.

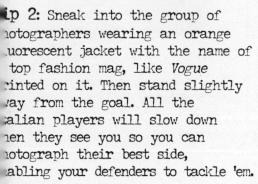

Tip 3: Get the stadium speakers to blast out some top, bangin, disco-type clubby toons, and ask the stadium electrician to get the floodlights to flash on and off, disco style. The Italians will think they are in a night-club, they'll rush over to one side, put on some sharp-looking clothes, comb their hair, suck in their cheeks a bit and frown at everyone. Don't ask me why, it's just what they do.

J is for...

Jail

As their guards watched the 1999 European Cup Final, two sneaky prisoners sneakily sneaked out of Sarajevo jail and escaped.

Jawbreaker

Alex Stepney once broke his jaw while playing for Manchester United . . . by yelling at his own players.

Jealousy

Supporting a football club can be really difficult if your town has two teams and you happen to support the rubbish one.

Manchester City and Everton FC have joined forces to offer counselling courses for coping with jealousy. 'We are world experts on coping with jealousy,' said a spokesman for both clubs before laying his head on my shoulder and weeping for twenty minutes.

Avoid the green-eyed monster.

Jim Johnson ... The Javelin

No.2 in a series of Unsung Footy Greats

Jim Johnson played for Wolves in the 1960s and had an unremarkable footy career until he had an accident on the treatment table. After suffering a back injury in a match against Arsenal, Johnson was left in traction. This is when they 'stretch' you on a table, a bit like the medieval torture rack. A forgetful nurse left Johnson's machine on for eight hours. Johnson went into hospital measuring 1.8 metres and left measuring 2.9 metres, so big he almost reached Niall Quinn's shoulders! He had been pulled into the distinctive 'javelin' shape which became his trade-mark. So thin he could hide behind goalposts at corners, springing out at the last moment to nod the ball home with his height advantage, 'The Javelin' notched an incredible 189 goals in 165 games.

JOBS

If you find that you are rubbish at footy but still want to be involved with a top-flight club, there are loads of jobs you can get behind the scenes. Here's a quick tour of some of the very best . . . and worst.

Footy Pie Maker

'Who Ate All The Pies?' is a light-hearted chant aimed at chubbier players. But what we at *The Ultimate A-Z of Footy* want to know is: who *makes* all those pies?

In fact, the job of Chief Pie Man is handed down from generation to generation, the secret recipes guarded closely by the Guild of Piemaking Brethren in their palatial Pie Lodge, where the legendary Worshipful Master's Book of Gravy is kept.

One way in, however, is to become a Pie Boy or Pie Girl, whose job is to ferret out some of the stranger ingredients that end up in the average footy pie: ferrets, for example.

Tooth Guard

It's a little-known fact, but almost all modern footballers are completely toothless, having had most of them knocked out by the hurly burly of the modern game. So, what do they do with all those sets of famous false teeth? They hand them over to the club Tooth Guard, that's what. You'll need a strong stomach (especially when dealing with the teeth of Craig Burley or Jaap Stam, for example), a working knowledge of dentistry and a very secretive nature (players need to know you won't let the *Daily Bilge* take photos of the spinach caught in between their molars).

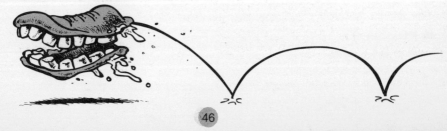

Celebrity Seat Warmer

With footy becoming more and more fashionable, clubs are attracting lots of top celebs who aren't used to the cold conditions at many football matches. And as the freezing-cold seats are obviously unsuitable for famous botties, today's club has realized the need for a Celebrity Seat Warmer, whose job it is to sit on the icy plastic until it has reached a temperature suitable for the bony bots of top super models. For this job you'll need some padding in the botty area yourself to insulate against the cold. It's also worth pointing out that this sort of work is only temporary, with there being little need for the Seat Warmer in the summer months (except in Scotland, obviously).

Tannoy Translator

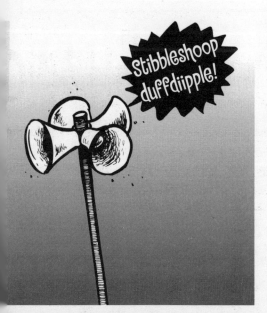

Stibbleshoop duffdiipple!

'Libferpoolsh fiiish, crackle, pop, spish, Manchsfersd Unnitere noo, Nerfacasartel, two . . .'

No one at footy grounds has ever been able to understand anything transmitted through the stadium sound system, known as the Tannoy. A Tannoy Translator's job is to mingle with the crowd and answer any questions they might have about the announcements. You'll have to train so that you are fluent in understanding the Tannoy. A six-month course is usually enough.

K is for...

Kilmarnock

Well, Kilmarnock just have to be in the 'K' section, don't they? They are the only UK side that begins with the letter 'K'. And that's about it for Kilmarnock.

Kangaroos

When teams play big games or friendly matches, they often exchange gifts like pennants, or flowers, or summat like that.

But surely the most useless gift ever given to a football team must have been the gift given to Czechoslovakian club Bohemians during a tour of Australia. They were given not one, but TWO live kangaroos. I mean, what were they supposed to DO with the things? Take 'em back to Czechoslovakia on the plane?

Knee

A bloke in the office, I mean a top footy boffin (they get around, don't they?) looked at how much wallop that a top footy player's knees get over a season. They calculated that it's equivalent to two elephants dancing the cha-cha on the knee. So here's a picture of what that would look like.

KRYPTONITE

Deadly rock and gas, giving off a nasty green glow which is the only substance that is harmful to Superman and is also used as a colouring ingredient in footy pie 'n' peas. Luvverly!

Kevin Keegan

Ex-England manager, Kevin 'I'm to Blame' Keegan, just seems to speak a language that comes from another world. Here's my personal Top Ten of the Thoughts of Chairman Kev:

'Goalkeepers aren't born today until they are in their twenties or thirties.'

Hmm.

'The thirty-three or thirty-four year olds will be thirty-six or thirty-seven by the time the next World Cup comes around if they're not careful.'

What?

'I know what is around the corner. I just don't know where the corner is. But the onus is on us to perform and we must control the bandwagon.'

Again, hmm.

'I don't think there's anyone bigger or small-er than Maradona.'

Er . . .

'It could be far worse for me if it was easy for me.'

'Scuse me?

'Argentina won't be at Euro 2000 because they are from South America.'

Well spotted, Kev.

'He can't speak Turkey, but you can tell he's delighted.'

Is English Kev's second language?

'It's understandable that people are keeping one eye on the pot and one up the chimney.'

Yes, you can't beat Kev when it comes to details.

'Young Gareth Barry: he's young.'

Eh?

'I'm not disappointed, just disappointed.'

You tell 'em, Kev.

Kissing!

Some of you have written to me about a problem that is becoming very troubling: **kissing after scoring a goal.**

It's a sad fact but there is no getting away from it: some of our top footballers do like laying the lips on one another during the game. It wasn't like that in my day I can tell you! No, when one of our manly forwards scored a goal he would simply accept a firm manly handshake from his teammates and trot, in a very manly fashion, back to the centre circle.

This sort of disgraceful scene can be seen across the country every Saturday afternoon.

When I watch one of today's modern matches I have to avert my eyes in the seconds following a goal. So, in an effort to stop this revoltingly unmanly behaviour, we have prepared some tips for those of you who are petrified after scoring a goal that you wi be forced to snog your teammates.

How to avoid being kissed after scoring:

Tip 1!

Don't brush your teeth for a few days before a big match and do develop bad personal hygiene (if you haven't got it already). One quick waft of your eggy breath up close will stop those simpering nellies getting too close.

Tip 2!

Don't stop running. After you've bagged the goal, simply keep legging it as fast as you can. Disguise your running as an over-the-top celebration. You only need to keep it up for a minute as the referee will then insist on the game being restarted.

Tip 3!

Before the game construct a small, camouflaged pit underneath both penalty spots, with a supply of food and water in each, and a submarine-style hatch. After scoring, pop open the hatch door, leap in, close the hatch and wait until things have calmed down and everyone has unpuckered their lips. Then slip out and rejoin the game.

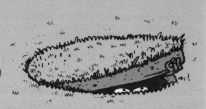

slaphead allows intelligent thoughts to escape bonce

extreeemely poor vision

insects live here

nasty-looking rash

undeveloped muscles due to being a total weedy wet

vile whiffy armpit pong

Lineker (Gary)

Bat-eared TV presenter who played for Leicester, Spurs, Barcelona and the mighty, mighty EV-ER-TON, EV-ER-TON, EV-ER-TON! Sorry, got a bit carried away for a mo' there.

Captained England and scored loads of goals (forty-nine) before packing it all in to flog crisps and be nasty to cuddly little Michael Owen.

Once described as 'the Queen Mother of English Football' by Vinnie Jones, Lineker played all his career without once being booked or sent off. Case closed.

LINESMAN!

Strange, ugly, oddly shaped, tree-dwelling creature of the night, feeds on small rodents, yukky insects and bits of old wood. Identified mainly by pasty skin, short legs, swollen belly, nasty little moustache, baldy comb-over head and almost **TOTALLY BLIND!** Yes! You know who you are, Arthur Mimms!!! That goal I got on Saturday was *NEVER* offside! Never!

Youwannagerrapairaspecs!!!!!

Oh all right, ref. Chatterton. C-H-A-T- . . .

Losing

When the other side scores more goals than you, you lose.
Simple, yes? Well, no. *Losing, real losing* is when England are in the 2000 European Championships, are 2-1 up with one minute left and Phil Neville (yes, we name the guilty men here) makes a meaningless lunge to give away a pen, when we only have to last another sixty seconds, and Romania (!) go through to the quarter-finals instead of us! Sob! *That's* losing.

Official England Euro 2000 bucket of tears

LUCK and David Beckham*

*Actually David Beckham doesn't appear in this bit . . . we just put that in to get your attention.

Luck plays a massive part in any football match. Footballers try as hard as possible to avoid bad luck by being among the most superstitious people who have ever walked the earth. Loaded up with enough lucky sprigs of heather to carpet Dartmoor, rabbit's feet by the truckload and more lucky coins than **Michael Owen**, yer average player leaps on to the pitch looking more like they are going to read your palm than belt one into the back of the net. **David Seaman*** takes it one stage further and takes to the pitch looking like a Mexican bandito. Surely the *only* reason for wearing that curious moustache ponytail combo is superstition? *See pages 94/95 for special Seaman offer!*

It's not just lucky knick-knacks either. **Paul Ince** famously keeps his shirt off until he gets on to the pitch (although this may have more to do with 'The Guvnor' thinking he looks the business without his shirt on . . .).

Sometimes players keep the same pair of lucky undercrackers on during a long cup run. Bearing in mind that a successful FA Cup run lasts from January to May, it's worth booking a downwind spot on the terraces from, say, the fifth round onwards. Of course, in some teams I've played for, some players just keep the same pair of undercrackers on for another reason: because they are dirty and exceptionally lazy.

The five amazing steps to Chatterton's lucky goal in the 1996 FA Cup Final

Step 3. Passing Venusian battle cruiser mistakes ref for the Evil Emperor of Galaxy 4.

Step 4. The sailor's favourite bird, the albatross, takes the rebound.

Step 5. It's in the back of the net!

Step 2. Unusually for someone so skilful, Chatterton wildly slices his volley. Fortunately he's wearing his lucky pair of undercrackers.

Step 1. 'Chopper' Higson tumbles over black cat.

The Strange Case of ...

Lawro's Tash!

Hound-faced ex-Liverpool superstar Mark Lawrenson once had a glittering career, picking up League titles, FA Cups and European Cups. When it all ended, Lawro turned to earning a living by being glum alongside Gary Lineker on *MOTD*. These days he occasionally gets a game with local park scufflers.

But in a shock exclusive, that has baffled scientists, we can reveal that Lawro's famous *moustache* has signed a four-year deal with Blackburn Rovers and will be playing a key role in central defence for the blue and whites.

'I played alongside Lawro for Liverpool,' said Rovers manager, Graeme Souness, 'and while I always thought Lawro had bags of talent, his tash was definitely one to watch for the future.'

Souness, himself fully tashed-up, sees Lawro's tash having no problems settling into top flight footy. 'It's all in the genes. Lawro had it in his DNA and now he's retired all that talent's been passed down the gene pool to his tash. Just don't ask me how it works!'

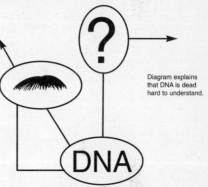

Diagram explains that DNA is dead hard to understand.

'Tashey' has already become a firm favourite in the Rovers' dressing room, despite an early run-in with centre forward, Matt Janssen.

'I thought the gaffer's dog had got loose in the dressing room,' laughed the striker, 'and I clobbered it with a mop! We are good mates now, though.'

Mark Lawrenson is rumoured to be selling the advertising space on his top lip to JJB Sports for a five-figure sum. He was unavailable for comment.

M is for...

Magic Sponge

It's a freezing January afternoon. The wind and hailstones are rattling your teeth and you've been hacked down by some nutter left back. What you *really* need is a kind, white-coated nurse to pat your hand and say 'There, there, ickle man.'

Yet, amazingly, this is not what happens when a player is injured. Instead, on rushes Alf, the trainer (they are always called Alf, or Ted, or Jim), carrying a bucket filled with grey sludge which he calls 'water' and a 'magic sponge' vibrating with bacteria and germs and radioactive waste. Before you can react, Alf whips out the sponge and plunges the freezing gloop straight down the back of yer neck. It doesn't do you any good at all, but you certainly don't stay lying down for long. Once, on one terrible occasion which I am still having sweat-soaked nightmares about, Alf sloshed the icy stuff straight down the front of my shorts.

MASCOTS

Footy teams love dressing some poor chump up in a fake-fur costume and letting them make a fool of themselves during the game. But sometimes we get a glimpse of the real animal underneath the outfit . . .

In a 1999 match at Rochdale, Halifax's Freddy the Fox got carried away with himself and pretended to pee on the Rochdale goalpost. He reckoned without Rochdale's own Desmond the Dragon who leaped onto Freddie and lamped him one. Police dragged the fiery Des away.

The FA took a dim view of another punch-up between Wolfie of Wolves (it just had to be, didn't it?) and Baggie Bird, the proud mascot of deadly Midland rivals West Bromwich Albion in a match at Wolves Molyneux Stadium in 1999.

Wolfie was also a key player in the all-time classic mascot dust-up. In 1998 Wolves played Bristol City. During the pre-game entertainment, Wolfie spotted three little pigs, representing, for some obscure reason, a double-glazing firm. Wolfie, obviously acting on instinct, tried to eat the three (not so little) pigs; or at least duff 'em up a bit. The fur really started flying when Bristol City mascot, City Cat, got involved. Stewards had to steam in and break up the beastly bout.

Motormouths!

Football and footballers aren't known for their brainpower. And if you don't believe us, just take a butcher's at this fine collection of footballing foot-in-mouth moments . . .

'I'm not convinced that Scotland will play a typically English game.'

Gareth 'The Miss' Southgate, Aston Villa

'I was alone up front, with Danny Murphy playing between me, myself and the midfield.'

Michael 'Just the Two of Us' Owen, Liverpool

'What will you do when you leave football, Jack, will you stay in football?'

Stuart 'Pink Shirt' Hall, TV reporter

'Alex Ferguson is the best manager I've ever had at this level. Well, he's the only manager I've actually had at this level. But he's the best manager I've ever had.'

David 'Tattoo' Beckham, Manchester United

'Germany are a very difficult team to play . . . they had eleven internationals out there today.'

Steve 'Ginge' Lomas, West Ham

'I'd like to play for an Italian club, like Barcelona.'

Mark 'Slaphead' Draper, Aston Villa

'Ian Baird is dashing round like a steam roller up front.'

Martin 'Big Coat' Tyler, Sky TV

'I've never wanted to leave. I'm here for the rest of my life, and hopefully after that as well.'

Alan 'Bus Pass' Shearer, Newcastle United

'The ball must be as slippery as a wet baby.'

Tony 'Strange Mind' Gubba, BBC TV

'The manager has given us unbelievable belief.'

Paul 'Brains' Merson, Aston Villa

'I dreamt of playing for a club like Manchester United, and now here I am at Liverpool.'

Sander 'Dazed and Confused' Westerveld, Liverpool

'I would not be bothered if we lost every game as long as we won the League.'

Mark 'The Spark' Viduka, Leeds United

'If it had gone in it would have been a goal.'

Barry 'The Tutter' Davies, BBC TV

'As the seconds tick down, Belgium are literally playing in time that doesn't exist.'

Guy 'Time Lord' Mowbray, TV commentator

'I was in Moldova airport and I went into the duty free shop - and there wasn't a duty free shop.'

Andy 'Let's Look at the Replay' Gray, Sky TV

Thanks to Simon @ The Football Quotes Page website for some of the quotes used.

N is for...

NASTY

Smiling Kenny Dalglish, the ex-Liverpool and Scotland player and ex-Liverpool, Blackburn, Newcastle and Celtic manager, was slightly less than charming after his Newcastle side were lucky to beat plucky little non-league Stevenage in a 1998 FA Cup replay. 'We wish them well in the FA Trophy . . . We hope they get beat in the next round.'

No Way! Yes, Way!

It's hard to believe but the 1919 clash between England and Scotland, usually one of the most violent games in the footy calendar, contained just FOUR fouls!

Ninety-Two Club

This club was formed with members made up of people who had watched a game at all ninety-two Football League grounds. Remarkable enough, but how about the feat of Alan Durban who, by 1976, had played at all ninety-two League grounds then in existence.

Nutters!

Are strange dangerous people. Nothing like Rick Thomas and his mate Trev Cole from Bristol, who locked themselves into a garden shed for the whole of the 2000 European Championship Finals so they could watch it all on TV.

Nutmeg

This is the most embarrassing thing you can do to a footballer, short of making him appear on stage at a Steps concert wearing a nappy and whistling the theme tune to *Neighbours*.

What is it? It's the art of 'the nutmeg', knocking the ball through an opponent's legs, then nipping past him to collect it on the other side. You'll find that yelling 'Megged yer, yer nugget!' as you do it adds lots of fun and jolliness to the manoeuvre. Unless someone does it to you, when it IS NOT FUNNY AT ALL

Nostradamus

No. 3 in a series of Unsung Footy Greats

Nostradamus was an ancient geezer who could predict the future. But did you know that he also played left back for Arsenal between 1974 and 1985? Well, he did, so there. What made Nostra, as he was known by his Gunner team-mates, so good a footy player was that he knew what was going to happen in the game *before it happened!* So, for example, if a player came bar-relling down the right wing towards him, Nostra would simply stand in the position where he knew he could take the ball off him. Things began to go wrong when Nostra stopped turning up for games he knew Arsenal would lose. 'There's nothing I can do about it,' he would say, 'so why bother?' The Arsenal manager ran out of patience with Nostradamus after the ancient sage deliberately gave away a penalty so that one of his predictions could come true.

O is for...

Off!

Wouldn't you have loved to have been at this game? When two top South American sides, Sportivo Ameliano and General Caballero, met in a league game played in Paraguay, referee William Weiler sent off TWENTY players! As this meant the Sportivo team were off the pitch, the match had to be abandoned. Referee Weiler would have got on famously with Mr Mike Woodhams who sent off all eleven members of the Juventus Cross team, plus some of their officials, in a 1973 cup match.

Not quite in the same league as Weiler and Woodhams is referee Mr Tarbet, who booked all eleven players plus two subs of the Glencraig youth team BEFORE they had left the dressing room. Mr Tarbet didn't like the chant that Glencraig were singing about him ...

Sometimes a player gets sent off but won't leave the pitch. In a 1956 'friendly' between Coventry City and San Lorenzo, from Argentina, Jose Sanfilippo of San Lorenzo kicked the ref and was sent off. The player refused to go and the ref had to abandon the game after only forty-four minutes had been played.

In a 1936 Olympic game between Italy and America, an Italian player was sent off but refused to go and, amazingly, was allowed to carry on playing! The US team reacted angrily and the game was abandoned.

offside

'Oi, ref! That was never offside' is the bleating call of the much-spotted duff striker. It can be heard every Saturday during the playing season at most grounds, professional and amateur, all around the country.

And what, exactly, is 'offside', eh? It's quite simple really. Right. If a player is in his own half when the ball is kicked forward they can't be offside but if they are in the opponent's half they are offside unless there is an outfield player between them and the goal when the ball is played or at least level with them and you can't be offside from a throw-in, I think, or if you step off the pitch or if you aren't interfering with the play or you are moving away from the goal or if there are two players running forward and the ball is played forward to the other player he isn't offside, I think, if he was not offside when the first player got the ball through or if it had been played by an opponent before the player touched it. Got that? Obvious really, isn't it?

As in 'Oi! Ref! that was never offside!'

You should never leave for a match without this handy word. Practise at home.

Old Invincibles.

Get this: how would you feel about a team from *Preston* who, *before* playing in the FA Cup Final, asked the referee to give them time to get their photo taken with the Cup, so confident were they of winning?

Cheeky blighters, you might say, and you'd have been right, cos they lost, 2-1, to West Bromwich Albion in the 1891 final. The nickname of the Preston side was 'The Old Invincibles' and they were the Manchester United of their time, sweeping almost all before them in the first ten years of the League.

OSTRICH

This is a picture of an ostrich.

This is a picture of Norwegian international, Tor Andre Flo.

1. Ostrich

2. Tor Andre Flo

There's no particular reason why we put these pictures next to each other. We just thought you'd like 'em.

Own Goals

Oh, the shame of it! You must know what it feels like, you stretch to make that last ditch clearance and, wallop, you've leathered the ball into your own net. What do you do? Well, the traditional response is simply to look at the goalie with a glare that should say '*Now look at what your poor positioning has made me do*'. However, if the goalie is flat on his back ten metres away, or you've actually chipped it over his head into the goal, you'll have to rely on some other excuses.

Here are a few of our suggestions:

'Mummy!'

'Oh, we're playing in *blue*?'

'Sorry, no speako da lingo.'

Of course, you can always take comfort from the fact that you aren't Jorge Nino, the Democrata player who scored THREE og's playing against Atletico Mineiro in 1982. Democrata lost 5-1. Or Pat Kruse of Torquay, who scored an og after just SIX seconds of a game against Cambridge United in 1977, the fastest og ever. Or Bob Stuart, who scored FIVE og's in one season while playing for Middlesbrough in 1935, the most ever scored by one player in a season. Chris Nicholl, playing for Aston Villa against Leicester City, scored all FOUR goals in a 2-2 draw in 1976.

P is for...

PENALTIES!

The 1987 Cup game between Aldershot and Fulham went to penalties. No fewer than twenty-eight penalties were taken before a winner could be found, with Aldershot beating Fulham 11-0.

In the 1903 season, Kettering's Fred Mearns saved NINETEEN penalties. Man City's Frannie Lee scored thirteen penalties in the 1972 season.

The whistle-happy ref gave FIVE penalties in the 1989 match between Crystal Palace and Brighton. THREE were missed.

Peter Noble, who played for Burnley between 1974 and 1979, scored TWENTY-SEVEN penalties in five years, without missing ANY.

The great Dutch player Johann Cruyff made the strange decision to PASS a penalty to a teammate in a game for Ajax against Helmond Sport in 1982. The player passed it back to Cruyff, who scored. Go figure.

In a 1998 Liverpool Premiership match, Robbie Fowler was given a penalty after falling over in the box. Despite him telling the referee it wasn't a penalty, the referee insisted it was. Fowler took a deliberately poor penalty which was saved by David Seaman in the Arsenal goal. Unfortunately for Arsenal, Fowler's Liverpool team-mate, Jason McAteer, wasn't so sportsmanlike and smashed the rebound straight in.

Penalty Shoot-out

Any England supporter (not to be confused with an Ing-er-land supporter) knows the misery that a penalty shoot-out brings. I still have teeth marks on my fingers after biting all my nails off watching England crash out of the 1998 World Cup.

But surely the weirdest ever penalty shoot-out was the one that took place in the 1890s between Leicester and, erm, an elephant. Four Leicester players were challenged to beat the elephant goalie using an oversized ball. Only one Leicester player, William Keech, managed to score against Jumbo.

Pop Music!

Aaaaaaaaargh! RUN FOR YOUR LIVES!!!!!!!!

It's a pop song sung by a footballer on the loose!!!!!

Let's face it, footballers and pop don't mix.

Let's take just one prime example. Andy Cole, the fabbo groovy Man U goal machine can do no wrong on t'footy pitch. But in 1998 he inflicted his 'rapping' on an unsuspecting nation with his bottom ten release 'Outstanding'. If you've ever wondered why he looks so fed up on the pitch, one listen will tell you all you need to know.

The lesson is easy: Footballers, if you are ever tempted to make a pop song . . . DON'T!

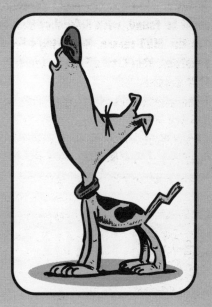

Ferenc Puskas of Hungary was one of the world's greatest ever players. The strange thing about Puskas was that he didn't look at all like a footballer. Here's a pic of him:

Puskas

As you can see, he doesn't look too dangerous, does he? That's exactly what some cocky English players thought when they turned up to play Hungary at Wembley in 1953: 'Look at that little fat chap there . . . we'll murder this lot,' said one player catching sight of Puskas.

The final score? England 3, Hungary 6. And it was no fluke. A year later, in a match in Hungary, Puskas was captain as the Hungarians beat England 7-1!

Q is for...

Queen's Park

Old amateur Scottish club, founded in 1867, who, throughout their entire history, have played in the professional leagues. Their home ground is the mighty Hampden Park, which has a capacity of 80,000. The average Queen's Park crowd is around 1,200. Back in the glory days, however, Queen's Park played seven seasons without losing. In five of those seasons they did not have a single goal scored against them!

Quick Quixall

Bert Quixall of Manchester United scored a goal after just FOUR seconds of a 1959 game against Bayern Munich. The same record is held by Bradford Park Avenue's Jim Fryatt for a goal against Tranmere in 1965. What makes Fryatt's goal so special is that FIVE Bradford players touched the ball before it hit the net!

Quiet Here, Isn't It?

Stockport County are used to crowds being small, but even they hoped for a few more for a 1921 match against Leicester, played at Manchester United's Old Trafford ground. The crowd? Thirteen.

Quit

Players get used to supporters pointing out the faults in their game. But in a game in 1942, Spurs player Andy Duncan got so fed up with it that he walked off the pitch in the middle of the game, quitting Spurs there and then. He never returned.

QUIZ!

Check your footy knowledge with our quick ten-question quiz . . .

1. Against which country did Michael Owen score his first-ever England goal?

2. Which two teams play at the San Siro Stadium?

3. How many times have England won the World Cup?

4. The famous black and white stripes of Juventus are based on the team shirts of which English club?

5. What does the word 'Real' in Real Madrid mean?

6. Against which top international side did tiny San Marino score the quickest-ever goal in international football after just fifteen seconds of a World Cup qualifying game?

7. At which ground do Scotland play their home games?

8. How many times have Brazil won the World Cup?

9. What was the fee paid by Newcastle United to Blackburn Rovers for Alan Shearer?

10. Which English club's nickname is The Toffees?

Answers: 1. Morocco 2. AC Milan and Inter Milan 3. Once, in 1966 4. Notts County 5. Royal 6. England 7. Hampden Park 8. Four 9. £15 million 10. Everton

R is for... ⚽ ⚽ ⚽

REFEREES!

Let's hear it for referees. God bless the little scamps, eh? Where would we be without these eagle-eyed, black-clad, wise owls of the pitch? And think of what they have to put up with . . .

Case 1 The ref in a Feb 2000 amateur game played in Shropshire sent off a player for swearing, only to see him return on to the field, this time driving at sixty miles per hour in his Peugeot 205.

Case 2 The assistant referee at a 1999 Liverpool v Aston Villa game, Wendy Toms, needed hospital treatment after the radio ear piece she used to keep in touch with referee Rob Harris, went wonky and screamed feedback into her ear.

Case 3 Ref Eddie Green, reffing a Ryman League game in October 1999, got so much stick during the first half that at half time he quit refereeing there and then, walking out of the ground.

All these sickening stories only prove what a tough job the Men (and Women) in Black do. Well, that's a point of view, I suppose.

Case 1 During a December 1995 game for Rangers v Hibs, the ref dropped his yellow card. Paul Gascoigne picked it up and, jokingly waved the card to 'book' the referee. However, referee Doug 'No Jokes Please' Smith booked Gascoigne.

Case 2 Even me, a hardened victim of some of the worst and most unjustified refereeing decisions in the history of footy, find this one hard to stomach. In a 1998 amateur game in the Bristol area, one of the players had only one arm, having lost the other in a work accident. While defending, the ball brushed against his empty sleeve, which was hanging loose and, you guessed it, the referee gives a penalty against the one-armed defender for handball.

Case 3 Melvin Sylvester refereed a game in Hampshire in 1998. Unfortunately he couldn't control himself, much less the game, and ended up punching one of the players. When Mel had had a chance to cool off he did the only thing he could do: he sent *himself* off and collected a six-week ban. Point proven, methinks.

RELEGATION!

Since Manchester United win all the time, the only excitement left to teams in the Premiership is if they get involved in a relegation battle. This has created an upside-down league championship which gets very exciting towards the end of the season. However, at *The Ultimate A-Z of Footy* we don't feel that there is enough motivation for players to avoid the dreaded drop, so we've come up with some ideas that add a bit more spice to each season's relegation clashes. Obviously we are only talking about the Premiership relegation battle. I mean, no offence, but who cares if Carlisle get relegated from Division 9 of the Northern Dr Martens Isthmian League?

Idea 1

On the final day of the season, specially constructed trap-doors will actually open beneath the feet of relegated players, plunging them straight into a two-metre-deep pit of rotten fish and cow poo. Serves 'em right, the overpaid nellies.

Idea 2

Force relegated teams to play in stiff, scratchy kits made out of old potato sacks. Only when they get promoted again can they get back into their soft, comfy shirts.

All relegated teams should be made to visit the home of every single supporter and apologize in person. The team should approach houses on their knees, wearing 'LOSER' signs around their necks.

Teams like Bristol City who, in the 1980s, became the first team to be relegated THREE times in a row, and who dropped eighty-six places in the league, should be disbanded, their grounds dismantled, the remaining rubble nuked, the players sold off for scrap and all mentions of the team wiped from computer databases.

Red Card

Gnarly Dean Windass picked up not one, but THREE red cards playing for Aberdeen against Dundee United in November 1997. The unlucky bruiser was sent for an early bath for picking up two yellow cards. He then moaned about it so much that the ref gave him a second red card. Dean hadn't finished and stopped on his way off the pitch to rip out the corner flag and hurl it, Zulu style, winning him his third red card. He picked up a six-week ban for the performance. That showed the ref, eh, Dean?

Colour and cut out for your very own red card!

S is for...

Slapheads!

No A-Z of footy would be truly complete without a quick razz around the wonderful world of footy slapheads. Unfortunately, due to modern hair-treatment methods available to today's well-paid balding professional, there just aren't the same number of gleaming bonces trotting out on to the pitch as there once were.

The magnificent, and now sadly all-too-rare, sight of the late evening sun glinting off the pate of a professional player. Alf-Inge Hoopla, trotting out for a 1972 game for Eindhoven v Frankfurt, bald as you like.

However, there i still a few notable baldies worth pointing out for y amusement. (Whil we are on the sub ject, reader A. N. Imaginarybloke wrote to us to po out that there is nothing very funn about the subject hair loss. Indeed, many men of you dad's age, it's a s sitive point and should be treated with respect and kindness. We've considered these points and would to say, 'Put a soc it, slaphead!')

Top Baldy player 1

Attilio Lombardo, Lazio and Italy. Properly baldy, Attilio flaunts his shining pate wherever he plays. He has looked as though he is around forty since he was twenty, which has helped him fool many a defender who can only watch flabbergasted as Lombardo sprints past them.

Top Baldy player 2

Steve Stone, Aston Villa and England. Bustling midfielder Steve has dealt with his thinning head by the 'shave-what-you've-got-to-disguise-your-slap' method.

Top Baldy player 3

Dion Dublin, Aston Villa and England. The classic approach also works for dashing Dion. He scores loads of goals with his completely gleaming, totally shaved bonce. No one actually knows if he is really bald or not!

SEAGULLS

Only two seagull stories here. The first is very boring. Brighton and Hove Albion's nickname is 'The Seagulls', cos they play by the seaside, geddit?

Much more interesting is the Strange Case of The Seagull Who Scored. A passing seagull managed to nod home a cross from thirteen-year-old Danny Worthington during a junior game in the Tameside Under-14 League. Ref Damian Whelan had no choice but to give the goal.

Silly Singing

'You only sing when you're winning ... you're not singing any more.'

Well, of course we aren't singing any more, you've just gone and scored, aintcha? Think about it. Why would anyone sing when they're losing?

SOUTH AMERICA!

Just for the hell of it, let's take a quick scoot around the wonderfully spicy world of Latin footy.

Brazil!

Obviously ace. Many times world champions, very fit, skilful, fast and good-looking (except for Ronaldo, maybe). The only problem I have with Brazil is that commentators go all drooly whenever they play. For example, many players who *aren't* Brazilian can take brilliant bendy free kicks and score often, for example David Beckham or Gianfranco Zola. Yet Roberto Carlos, the Brazilian full-back, took one free kick years ago and scored and since then you'd think that no one else on the planet ever scored a free kick. He's never done it again either, taking all Brazil's and Real Madrid's free kicks and blurting them up into Row ZZ at The Maracana Stadium.

But commentators look at anything the Brazil team do, including walking, and say 'Oh! You have to say that is wonderful! Silky samba carnival fiesta 1970 Pele blah de blah de blah . . .' Nobody mentions how utterly useless they were against France in the 1998 World Cup Final, famous for Ronaldo's imitation of a zombie. Pah!

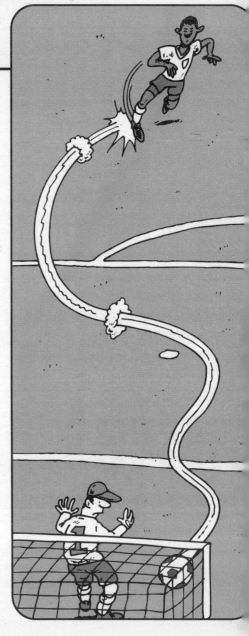

Argentina!

Also very good but not quite as good as they used to be since Maradona (that's Maradona, the podgy ex-Best Footballer in the World, not to be confused with Madonna the American singer) packed it in. Top stars: Crespo, Veron and Batistuta.

Colombia!

Also famous for mad goalies, including my personal fave mad keeper, Rene Higueta who made the famous 'Scorpion' save against England in 1995 . . .

Mexico!

Is actually in Central America so doesn't count really.

Uruguay!

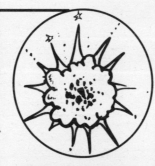

Famous in the past for being dead good at footy, winning two World Cups and thirteen South American Championships. Now really famous for being very, er, 'excitable' during games.

Chile!

Pretty good. Mad goalies.

Peru!

The most famous Peruvian player is called Norberto and plays for Newcastle.

All the other teams are rubbish but very, very entertaining to watch. Not for the footy, obviously, but for the incredible fouls they all go in for.

T is for...

Translation

Football people speak another language, as we saw on pages 58/59. So we've prepared a quick guide to help you understand the after-match interview.

Footy Phrase	Translation
'Sick as a parrot, Brian.'	'I was very disappointed with the outcome of the game so much that my appearance may resemble that of an unwell exotic bird, Brian.'
'Over the moon, Brian.'	'I am very pleased with the outcome of the game, so pleased, in fact, that I feel like I could leap over the large lunar sphere orbiting the earth, Brian.'
'We was robbed, Brian.'	'In my opinion we were deprived of a result that should rightfully have declared us the winners, Brian.'
'The ref was a disgrace, Brian.'	'The match official fell some way short of the standards I expected in his performance today, Brian.'

Time

We've discovered an astonishing change to the normal laws of science: footy time.

In footy time, when your team is winning 1-0, time expands so that each minute added-on turns into 765,456,000 seconds and it's perfectly possible to grow old, raise a family and retire to a nice little bungalow in the three extra 'minutes' the ref has played. On the other hand, if you are a fan of the other side, with only three minutes *left* to score before being relegated, those minutes will compress into less than a nanosecond (that's a very small measurement of time) and all play will scream by in a blinding flash.

TimeWastingTed

No. 4 in a series of Unsung Footy Greats

Ted Fripp played 236 games in a ten-year career for Everton during the 1970s. He had no football skills . . . except one. Ted was always a substitute and was only called on during the last few minutes of vital games when Everton were clinging on to a narrow lead. The reason? Ted was an expert in time wasting. Ted had been dropped on his head as a baby on to a football, leaving him with a ball shaped groove on top of his bonce. All Everton had to do was to chip the ball up on to Ted's head and let him stand there while the opposition tried to get it back. Thanks to Ted's incredible height and his vast bulk, no player could ever dislodge the ball once it was up on his head and time could play out for Everton.

U is for...

UEFA!

(Utterly Evil Football Association!)

UEFA (The Union of European Football Associations), as we know and love it, make all the important decisions about European footy.

But not many people know that there is another, sinister UEFA we need to warn you about: the *Utterly Evil Football Agency*.

It's a secretive organization which is plotting to destroy football for ever from their secret headquarters inside an active volcano in Switzerland. The leader of UEFA (the evil UEFA, not the dead good UEFA), Ernst Blowfootball, has plans to blow up the world next Tuesday unless all the world's leaders give in to his evil demands to make the goals smaller, make everyone offside all the time and to bring back Glenn Hoddle to manage England.

Dr Blowfootball

nly one man can save the world:
renton Park, top-secret British
gent and attacking midfielder.

Armed with only a set of net
pegs, some shinpads and a secret
radio watch, Park scales the
walls of the UEFA volcano using
the pegs, abseils into Ernst
Blowfootball's meeting and
secretly substitutes a fine
upstanding British rule-book for
the nasty UEFA one. Hurrah!

otball has been saved and Prenton Park escapes
a rocket-powered jetskihelicopterplanecar
ingy after blowing up the UEFA HQ.

THE UNDEAD!

Oh, yes. The Undead, the Zombies are amongst us. Strange sightings of these creatures from another world have been reaching our desk from around the globe. They can be spotted easily by the 'dead fish' eyes, the lumbering, heavy-legged run, the icy breath and the fact that they all play in central defence.

Jaap Stam, Martin Keown, Lucas Radebe, Sammi Hyppia. All top-class players no doubt. All nice, pleasant, well-adjusted individuals, kind to their families and dogs.

But Flesh-eating Zombies, every last one of 'em!

Check out Martin Keown's eyes next time he's making a 'tackle'. If they aren't the staring eyes of a visitor from The Underworld then I don't know what I'm talking abou

Wait a mo', just realized that I *don't* know what I'm talking about, so scrub that last bit. Sorry, Martin! Please don't come round and lurk at me menacingly.

Unlikely Scoreline

It's depressing, isn't it, when your favourite team is getting a whuppin'? Imagine how fed up the supporters of Charlton Athletic were in a game played in December 1957 against Huddersfield Town. Charlton, playing at home, were 5-1 down against the visitors. Not only that, they had been down to ten men since the tenth minute and now there were only thirty minutes left. Some Charlton supporters left early.

But one Charlton player, Johnny Summers (great name, sounds more like a rock star!) changed his boots, moved up to centre forward and scored four goals in a fifteen-minute blitz. Charlton scored another to make it 6-5 before Huddersfield scored again. At 6-6, Charlton scored in the last minute to win, 7-6! ELEVEN goals had been scored in the second half . . .

UNBELIEVABLE!

It's UNBELIEVABLE! that . . . Chelsea sacked Gianluca Vialli after winning four trophies in four seasons.

It's UNBELIEVABLE! that . . . France won the World Cup in 1998 and the European Championship in 2000 and England didn't.

It's UNBELIEVABLE! that . . . Everton aren't as good as Man Utd.

It's UNBELIEVABLE! that . . . I never got picked to play for England and in fact sometimes didn't even get picked to play for North Freckleton's Under-15 third team.

United States of America

The place where footy becomes 'sarker' and where they play around with the rules of our glorious game. But before we get too snooty about the Americans, let's remember that in 1993 they beat England 2-0 fair and square.

83

V is for...

Virtual Footy!

In this spanking new sparklysilveryspangly super future we all live in now, there's absolutely no need to go and get yourself cold, wet and dirty by actually *playing* footy. No sir, with this spiffy virtual reality footy kit, you can simply slump back in yer armchair and away you go . . .

nlike normal footy comput-
r games, Virtual Footy
rings the actual experience
f playing the game right
to your living room
rough top-notch
lographic techno gizmo
:uff. For example, you can
ug yourself into any
me, from any period of
oty history and be any
ayer you like!

Fancy seeing how Michael Owen would
play if you picked him as right back in a
Division 3 mud'n'blood special? Or go
further and add characters from history
to famous games. You could be Genghis
Khan playing in midfield for Manchester
United against Liverpool . . . or get Albert
Einstein (whaddya mean who? Look it up,
yer dingbat) turning out between the
sticks for Napoli against the Faroe
Islands.

'Upside down' mode you can
verse roles and see what
ppens when you put
otballers in famous situations
m history. For example, how
out seeing how Dwight Yorke
pes with landing on the moon,
see what happens when Kevin
illips leads the American
oops into battle during the
ttle of the Bulge! It's a riot!

rder now to avoid disappointment: only £1,435,689.99

Vroom!

A nasty Chelsea hooligan was busy throwing stones at coaches containing Middlesbrough supporters heading back for the long drive home after a game at Stamford Bridge in 1995. One of the coaches stopped and dragged the hooligan aboard. They then drove the 230 miles back to Middlesbrough and dropped the little twerp off at the side of the road . . .

The Valley and The Night of the Living Dead

Don't hang around late at night after paying a visit to Charlton Athletic's home ground The Valley. When it was first built, it was built in an old chalk pit. The terraces were made from soil dug from the grounds of an old hospital. This soil contained bones from real live dead people! Oo-er!

Violence

Football violence is a terrible, terrible thing. Just listen to what happened at a game between a team from Cambridge University and a team from nearby Chesterton. The game had not been on for long when quarrels between the teams broke out. The Chesterton team left the pitch and came back armed with lengths of wood they had hidden in a nearby church porch. They attacked the Cambridge team, wounding many and leaving many with broken bones. We don't know if the police got involved because the game took place in 1581 . . .

(The) Vulcan Stun Grip and ....
The Alan Hansen Mind Meld!

Fans of the old *Star Trek* series will know all about Mr Spock from the planet Vulcan and his Vulcan Stun Grip. All Spock has to do is to lightly grip a secret spot on yer shoulder and, biff! Down you go like a sack of spuds, unconscious.

But did you know that the deathly pale, BBC *Match Of The Day* celebrity commentator Alan Hansen has exactly the same skill? Alan has actually taken the Vulcan Stun Grip a stage further by not needing to touch you to let you have it! Hansen, clearly descended from a long line of Vulcans (think about it; like Vulcans he shows no emotion, believes in logic, looks like he's never seen the sun, let alone been out in it), only has to start speaking and I slump to the floor, completely sparko. Some people have claimed that I simply fall asleep through boredom but that couldn't possibly be true, could it, because Alan Hansen is one of the most respected and witty TV commentators in the world.

Verona

Verona play in Italy and recently built a new stadium. They wanted to name it in the traditional way, after a famous dead ex-Verona player. They picked Aldo Olivieri, a star from an Italian World Cup-winning team. Everything was set for the ceremony when it was discovered that Aldo was in fact alive and well at the age of eighty-six. Oops.

WHISTLE Happy Day!

As we have seen earlier in this mighty, mighty book, refs are on the receiving end of a ridiculous amount of stick from gobby managers and ignorant crowds every Saturday (and Sunday, Monday, Tuesday, Wednesday and Thursday).

So, what we are launching is 'Whistle Happy Day', a charity day for all referees. What we want to happen is this: on a particular Saturday (which we haven't decided on yet) all players, spectators and managers will be very nice to the men in black.

In case you're wondering exactly how this whizzo scheme will work we've prepared these three examples of what might happen on 'Whistle Happy Day' . . .

Example 1

On 'Whistle Happy Day' Roy Keane is clean through on goal after a ten-man move from defence. It's the last minute of the Premiership decider and United *need* that goal. Keane gets a slight knock but it doesn't put him off. It's a clear case for playing an advantage. But referee Clifford Difford blows his whistle for a free kick to United! However, instead of eating Clifford alive, Roy trots over, gives him a smile and says, 'The referee's decision is final and I cheerfully accept it in the spirit it was given, Mr Difford.'

Example 2

On 'Whistle Happy Day', Ecuador are playing El Salvador in a crucial Copa America tie. Referee Manuel Labour disallows a goal by El Salvador. Normally this would signal the start of a small South American war at the very least. However, as it's 'Whistle Happy Day', the players and crowd content themselves with simply dismantling the stadium and chasing Manuel deep into the rainforest where he remains for eight years living on jumbo bugs and monkey scraps.

Example 3

On 'Whistle Happy Day', author/illustrator/amateur footy star Martin Chatterton needs only one more goal to top last season's tally of 245. With the clock ticking he beats eight men and leathers the ball past the keeper from ninety metres out. Referee Ken Doo disallows the goal and I end up serving a twenty-two-month ban for giving Ken a right mouthful. 'Whistle Happy Day' or no 'Whistle Happy Day', there ARE limits.

Water-logged Pitch

The astonishing 1999 game between Birkdale Rovers and Southport Trinity abandoned in the seventy-fifth minute.

WINGEF

In your parents' day, a 'winger' was a player who played in attack on either side of the pitch, near to the touchline. Usually these players had great ball skills and speed. Ryan Giggs is a good example of someone who would have been called a winger back in them olden days. But did you know that the name 'winger' was used because, during World War Two, bored bombe pilots played footy on the huge wings of Lancaster bombers to pas: the time on long flights?

World Cup Upsets

The history of the World Cup is that the big teams usually win, but there have been many amazing performances by unfancied teams.

The USA beat England 1-0 in the 1950 Finals at a time when England were considered unbeatable.

Cameroon beat Argentina 1-0 in the opening game of the 1994 World Cup.

However, the all-time title of World Cup Giantkillers must go to the 1966 North Korea team. Playing their games at Goodison Park, Everton's ground, the Koreans were popula with the locals. They had done reasonably well in the first two games, losing 3-0 to Russia and drawing 1-1 with Chile. In the third game they were given no hope against Italy, who were tipped for the title. Korea won 1-0, sending Italy out (the team was pelted with tomatoes on arrival back in Italy). North Korea played another top Europea side in the quarter finals and stunned everyone by racing into a 3-0 lead. Portugal, lec by the legendary Eusebio, hit back in a classic match and eventually won 5-3, ending North Korea's wonderful World Cup run.

WAGES

It's unbelievable, isn't it, what all these prancing prima donna footballers get paid these days? In my day, football blokes only got thirty-two pence a year *and* had to pay for their own half-time tea. Now they're all on a gazillion pounds a game, driving solid gold cars and wearing diamond-encrusted under-crackers, aren't they? And the houses! All of them players, even the rubbish ones (and they're all rubbish, aren't they? Not like in my day when we had *real* players like Alf Spit who could dribble like a wizard), own castles and palaces with lots of toilets and have 305 servants, including a man who is just there to brush their teeth and another one whose job is just to sweep up the loose hundred-pound notes that drift around the mile-long, marble-lined corridors.

We should put them all in the army. That'd sort them out.

Recent pictures prove that modern players do, in fact, have money coming out of their ears.

Wobble

No Ultimate A-Z of Footy would be complete without us doffing our flat caps to the greatest ever English goalie, William 'Fatty' Foulkes. The mighty chubster kept goal for Sheffield United and England in the early 1900s and weighed in at 140 kilos!!!!

He was able to carry a grown man under each arm, once scoffed all ELEVEN of his team's breakfasts before they had a bite, snapped a crossbar during a game, chased a referee around around the Crystal Palace grounds and, when injured, could only be carried from the pitch by six men. Now imagine Fatty Foulkes in today's game. Could you really see him joining David James on the fashion catwalk?

Who Are You?

The Manchester United team line-up for the photo before the 2001 European Champion's League quarter-final tie against Bayern Munich was a familiar one to any football fan: Keane, Brown, Stam, Silvestre, Giggs, Neville, Cole . . . and Karl Power. Who?

Karl Power, an unemployed labourer and Man United fan, tricked his way onto the official team photo by simply turning up, in full United strip, walking over and standing next to Andy Cole. Despite the terrifying risk of being caught by Roy Keane, Karl managed to pull off one of the best stunts in modern footy.

Who Are You 2?

But Kunning Karl isn't the only trickster the game has seen. When Graeme Souness was managing Southampton he signed a player called Ali Dia on a month's contract. Souness signed the player after getting a call from George Weah, the former World Footballer of the Year and AC Milan star. However, the caller wasn't Weah and Dia was a complete fake! He managed to get on as a substitute against Leicester City and Souness discovered his mistake . . . Dia was totally rubbish! He was quickly substituted and hasn't been heard from since.

Wallop!

Big scores are nothing new but in recent years, as modern defences get tighter, mad scores have become rare. So we are delighted to report on Australia's 2002 World Cup qualifier against Tonga. The Aussies chalked up a magnificent TWENTY-TWO goals against the Tongans. Not content with that performance they played American Samoa a few days later and won 32-0. Top tonking cobber!

Wigged Out!

In an effort to shake off their 'least glamorous club in England' tag, Preston North End show off their latest signing, George P. Clinton and his big wig.

And talking of wigs, turn over the page to get a completely fabtastical FREE GIFT from us kind-hearted cheapskates at *The Ultimate A-Z of Footy!*

A-Z Special Free Gift!

At last! By popular demand, all of us kind-hearted dudes down at *The Ultimate A-Z of Footy* have come up with this superfootastic 'David Seaman Virtual Reality Simulator'!

Simply cut around the shapes, and follow the easy-to-understand instructions and you too will soon have that oh-so-fashionable Seaman barnet! Until recently this kind of simulation technology was only available to rich bods and other smarmy twerps. But now, thanks to US, everyone has the chance to be David Seaman.

Go on, you know you want to!

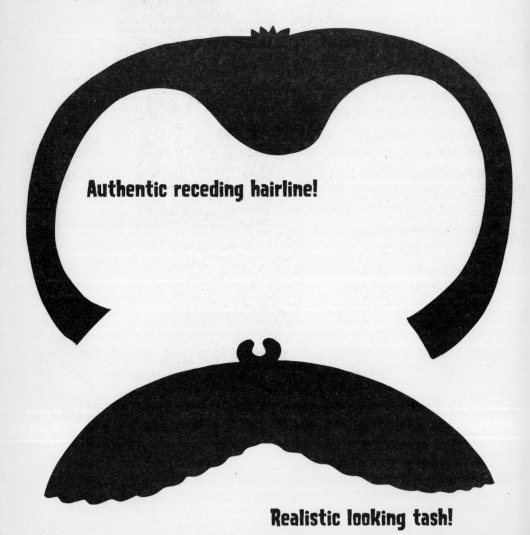

Authentic receding hairline!

Realistic looking tash!

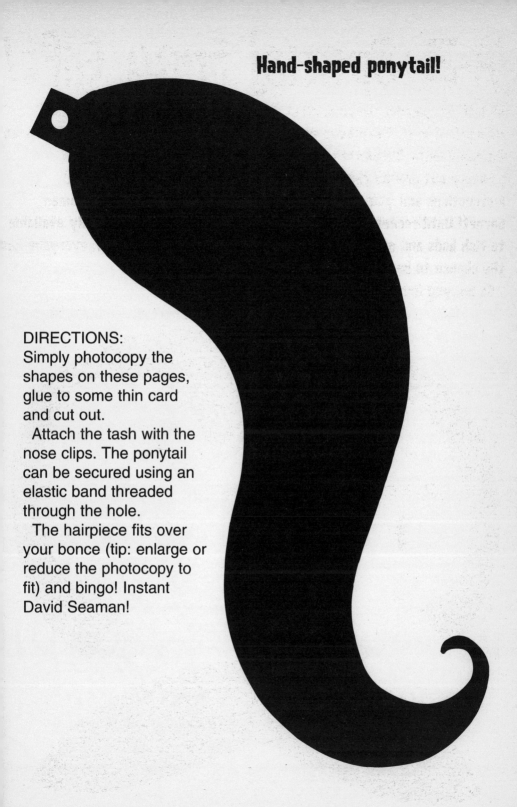

DIRECTIONS:
Simply photocopy the
shapes on these pages,
glue to some thin card
and cut out.
   Attach the tash with the
nose clips. The ponytail
can be secured using an
elastic band threaded
through the hole.
   The hairpiece fits over
your bonce (tip: enlarge or
reduce the photocopy to
fit) and bingo! Instant
David Seaman!

X is for...

X-rated Tackles!

Can we ask all small children, expectant mothers and those of a nervous disposition to leave this book while we look at our collection of the worst-ever tackles in football history.

Have they gone? Very well, let's draw back the curtains and look at this Hall Of Horrors...

X-Rated Tackle 1

Bolton Wanderers' American defender Holdem Tightly had to be pieced together by a ten-strong team of surgeons when he exploded into 435 pieces after this outrageous tackle by West Ham's Brazilian left back Ansa Da Fone.

Mrs Brenda Pile hoovers up the bits of Tranmere Rovers' Canadian striker Sloppy Fudge, left after he had been liquidized by opponent Trimford Nugent in a 1997 Worthington Cup second round, second-leg game against non-League side, Atletico Tharp Doofer FC.

Liverpool's fearsome Scottish full back Grimly Fiendish leaves a deep trench in wet conditions when making this hideous sliding tackle on Everton's dainty central midfielder Havabitta Bunloaf Sid.

Xylophone

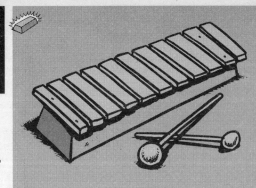

As far as I know, xylophones have absolutely no place in the wonderful world of footy, but we are on the letter 'X' so what do you expect? 'X' is *always* for 'xylophone'.

X Marks the Spot

The 'Spot the Ball' competition is the one in newspapers where you have to look at a photo of a footy match where the ball has been cleverly taken out of the picture and guess where it should have been. Tricky, eh?

However, in February 1995, the *Peterborough Evening Telegraph* had thousands and thousands of winners who had all put their crosses in exactly the right spot . . . mainly because the paper had forgotten to take the ball out of the picture.

Xtra Time

Ok, it's a bit of a cheat but I gotta fill this page somehow, haven't I? So here's a couple of dead-good Xtra Time facts.

Ref Clive Thomas once added on a monster forty-five minutes of extra time (strictly speaking, this is really called 'time added on' but I don't care. It's my book, so yah boo sucks) in a match played on a sloping pitch. The reason for the time added on was that the ball had run down the slope so many times.

In 1962 a match between Penarol and Santos in the Copa Libertadores lasted more than three and a half hours, about two hours extra time having been played!

Xavier, Abel

Come on, we're on the letter 'X' here so we are obviously going to poke a bit of fun at the ever-changing haircuts of Portuguese midfielder, Abel Xavier, surely the weirdest-looking player ever to take to a football pitch. Here's a quick run through some of Amazing Abel's haircuts down the years . . .

1

Yer standard blond bombshell Abel

2

Leaning Tower of Pisa

3

Mission to Mars

4

Sea Urchin

 # X-Ray Spex!

Check out this fantastic new bit of kit. With 'X-Ray Spex' we can get a glimpse through the clothes of top players . . . and we found out some interesting things!

Fashion plate Becks in dodgy undercracker shock!

Fabian Barthez keeps paperback novels in his socks to prevent boredom!

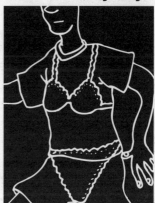

For obvious reasons we cannot reveal the identity of this top player.

Y is for...

YETI!

This secret film, taken at my old school by a cameraman disguised as a tree, shows a shadowy figure lumbering towards the goal. If you look closely at the footage you will see that his face, legs and hands have been shaved and a layer of fake 'skin' added. Whenever his shirt is pulled back from his wrist or back you can quite clearly see that he is covered in a thick mat of dark fur . . .

There's only one possible explanation. The seemingly innocent PE teacher taking Form 3B for afternoon footy is, in fact, the half human, half beast otherwise known as the 'Yeti' or 'Bigfoot'! We'd advise you all to check out your sports teachers for the tell-tale signs and let us know if they are the Missing Link that scientists have been looking for, oh, absolutely yonks.

Yellow Card

Playing for Sheffield United, Vinnie Jones got booked after only FIVE seconds of a game against Manchester City in 1991. He repeated this amazing feat the following season when playing for Chelsea against . . . Sheffield United.

Early experiments with the yellow card proved unsuccessful

Youth

The youngest player to score in an FA Cup Final was Norman Whiteside, for Man Utd against (sob!) Everton, at the tender age of eighteen years and fourteen days. He was also Northern Ireland's youngest ever international, making his debut against Yugoslavia at the age of seventeen years, forty-one days.

Bert Geldard in 1927, and Ken Roberts in 1951, both made their league debuts at exactly the same age: fifteen years and one hundred and fifty-eight days.

Michael Owen became the youngest ever England goalscorer when he notched one in his first game against Morocco in 1998 at the age of eighteen years, eighty-six days.

YIKES!

If you go and watch Betis Seville in Spain, take care where you sit. One fan who goes to every game is, gulp, dead! The dead fan's ashes are taken in a jar to all Betis's games by his son, and shaken every time Betis score!

Zola and the Micro Man

Gianfranco Zola, the titchy little Italian striker, is even smaller in reality than he is on TV. In fact he is no bigger than a small dog, say a cocker spaniel or a border collie.

Arno pictured with actual boot

However, Gianfranco is not the smallest player ever to play at the highest level. No, according to extensive research what we didn't do, that honour goes to Arno Van Der Graafgenerator, the Dutch midfielder who played for Ajax in the late 1970s. Arno was little more than thirty-five centimetres tall and was a devastating midfield general. Equipped with a UEFA-approved voice amplifier, squeaky-voiced Arno could make himself heard in any crowd. He had to retire from the game when he was unintentionally smashed into the crossbar. In the unfortunate incident, Arno had sheltered behind the match ball during a hailstorm thinking the game had been stopped, when up stepped Bobby Charlton and leathered the ball (and Arno) against the crossbar . . .

Zigger Zagger!

An ancient football chant which was once used as the title of a play about, er, football chants. 'Zigger Zagger Zigger Zagger Zigger Zagger' goes the chant, keeping it right up there with 'Oggy Oggy Oi!', 'Wey-Oh-Wey-Oh-Wey, Oh Wey, Oh Wey!', 'Na Na Na Na, Na Na Na Na, Hey He-ey, Liverpool (or whoever you happen to support)!', "Ere We Go, 'Ere We Go, 'Ere We Go!', 'Ooh-Ah Cantona, I said Ooh-Ah Cantona!' and the 1998 World Cup smash, 'Na Na Na, Na Na Na, Na Na Na Na Na Na!', or 'Vindaloo' as it was more commonly known. Classics, all of 'em, I think you'll agree.

Zimmer Frame

We know that for you wet-behind-the-ears sprogs that anyone over the age of fifteen is considered to be a wrinkly pensioner. However, it's a fact that many players are keeping going longer and longer, sometimes carrying on at the highest level until they are an ancient thirty-eight, even thirty-nine. You may be surprised to know that in 1965 Stanley Matthews played his last game for Stoke City at the age of FIFTY! Even that was beaten by Neil McBain of New Brighton (who were then in the Football League) who played as goalie when he was fifty-two years old!!!!

More recently, forty-two-year-old John Lukic turned out for Arsenal after three years out of the team to keep goal in a vital European game against Lazio. At the amateur level, the Mobile Wrinkly Award goes to Jack Wattam who, after more than 5,000 games, was still playing when he was seventy-four ...

Lukic had not expected the call-up . . .

Zadly

Not an Albanian international . . . zadly, it's the end of the book. Almost.

The End

Thanks to everyone who helped with the making of this book. It was mainly *me*, of course, but one or two other people did help a little so thanks go out to Ann Chatterton, Amanda Li, Jacqui McDonough, Leah Thaxton, Eoghan Lynch, everyone at Greenbank on Thursday nights, Everton FC (for staying up) and to everyone at Sandpiper Greens.

I'd also like to point out that all references to anyone alive, dead, or anything in between are all purely for fun and I didn't mean it really, so please don't hit me.

index

Aldershot 66
Aldis, Peter 38
American Samoa 93
Arbroath 36
Argentina 77, 90
Arsenal 66, 103
Aston Villa 38, 65
Australia 93

Barcelona 52
Barthez, Fabian 34
Bartram, Sam 31
Beckham, David 5, 6, 8, 58, 76
Beresford, John 35
Bergkamp, Dennis 7
Birmingham City 4
Bon Accord 36
Bosnich, Mark 34
Botham, Ian 9
Bradford Park Avenue 68
Brazil 76
Bremner, Billy 6
Brighton and Hove Albion 30, 38, 66, 75
Bristol City 57, 73
Brolin, Tomas 25
Burnley 66

Cameroon 90
Carlisle United 7
Carlos, Roberto 76
Charlton, Jack 6
Charlton Athletic 31, 83, 86
Chile 35, 77
Cole, Andy 67
Colombia 77
Corinthians 36
Coton, Tony 20
Coventry City 9, 62
Cruyff, Johann 66
Crystal Palace 66
Cullis, Stan 12

Dalglish, Kenny 60
Davison, Aidan 23
Democrata 65
Dia, Ali 92
Doncaster Rovers 25
Draper, Mark 59
Dublin, Dion 75
Duncan, Andy 68
Durban, Alan 60

Edmilson 14
England 90
Everton 23, 44, 52

Ferguson, Alex 26
Forfar Athletic 31
Foulkes, William 90
Fowler, Robbie 66
France 83
Fryatt, Jim 68
Fulham 66

Gascoigne, Paul 71
Geldard, Bert 101
General Caballero 62
Giggs, Ryan 90
Grimsby Town 11
Grobelaar, Bruce 35

Hadji, Moustapha 9
Halifax 57
Hansen, Alan 87
Hereford United 9
Hibernian 7
Higueta, Rene 77
Honved 12
Howard, Fred 20
Huddersfield Town 83
Hungary 67
Hunter, Norman 6

Ince, Paul 53
Ipswich Town 42
Italy 43, 62, 90

Jansen, Matt 55
Jones, Vinnie 52, 101

Keane, Roy 6
Keegan, Kevin 49
Kettering 66
Kilmarnock 48
Kruse, Pat 65

wrenson, Mark 54, 55
Boeuf, Frank 5
e, Francis 66
cester City 52, 65, 66
eker, Gary 52
erpool 11, 35, 66
mas, Steve 58
mbardo, Attilio 75
kic, John 103

Ateer, Jason 66
nchester City 44, 66
nchester United 11, 26, 34, 38, 92
radona, Diego 24, 77
tthews, Stanley 103
arns, Fred 66
rson, Paul 59
xico 77
ddlesbrough 65
ton, Steve 21
scow Spartak 12
rray, Dennis 21

ville, Phil 52
wcastle United 30, 60
choll, Chris 65
ho, Jorge 65
ble, Peter 66
rth Korea 90
ttingham Forest 30

ven, Michael 5, 101
ford United 24

nalties 36, 66
nnington, Jessie 11
ru 77
rtugal 90
eston North End 36, 63, 93
skas, Ferenc 67

een's Park 68
ixall, Bert 68

dford, Ron 9
du, Ion 9
msey, Alf 42
ading 24
erees 16, 25, 52, 62, 70-1, 88
id, Peter 15
a, Carlos 24
berts, Ken 101
bson, Bobby 42
chdale 57
jas, Roberto 35
naldo 11, 76

Sanfilippo, Jose 62
Schmeichel, Peter 33
Scotland 31
Scunthorpe United 9
Seaman, David 53, 66
Shearer, Alan 59
Sheffield United 90
Sheffield Wednesday 30
Shrewsbury Town 14
Smith, Alan 6
Smith, Gordon 39
Souness, Graeme 55, 92
Southampton 92
Southgate, Gareth 58
Sportivo Ameliano 62
Stepney, Alex 44
Stevenage 60
Stockport County 25, 68
Stoke City 103
Stone, Steve 75
Stuart, Bob 65
Summers, Johnny 83
Sunderland 38
Surnam, Les 21

Tabbia, Francesco 34
Taibi, Massimo 24
Thomas, Clive 25, 98
Tonga 93
Torquay United 65
Tottenham Hotspur 52
Trautmann, Bert 34

Uruguay 12, 77
USA 62, 83, 90

Van der Gouw, Raymond 34
Verona 87
Vialli, Gianluca 24, 83
Viduka, Mark 21, 59
Viera, Patrick 6

West Bromwich Albion 11, 12, 57, 63
West Ham United 4
Westerveld, Sander 59
Whiteside, Norman 101
Windass, Dean 73
Wolverhampton Wanderers 12, 57

Xavier, Abel 99

Zola, Gianfranco 76, 102

This is a special announcement for all visiting readers.
Please proceed to the exits in an orderly fashion.

We would ask you to remember that this is a residential area and to refrain from chanting. Also remember to check you have all your belongings and to ensure you keep your ticket stub for forthcoming books.

Outside the book, transport has been arranged to take you back to reality. The coaches are parked in the Elton Welsby Memorial car park and are clearly marked. Make sure you are on the correct vehicle as we cannot be responsible for spectators who are deposited in an alternative reality. Thank you for visiting and for your patience.